A valuable source of information by someone who works in the trenches. Whether you or a loved one are currently facing challenges, or if you simply want to be prepared for what you may face in the future, this provides the necessary tools. Knowledge is power.

Steve Fairfax, Currently helping my neighbor who has dementia

Diane answers questions most of us have not even thought of but desperately need to know. You will find valuable insight into the later years of life.

Dr. Jim Gwinn, Former President, CRISTA Ministries

As accountants, we can crunch the numbers. But Diane has outlined many issues we would never know, but which clearly need to be considered. This is an important resource in understanding key senior living issues.

Craig Huish, CPA, Waterfront CPA Group

A must-read for all dealing with aging. It debunks the myth that staying in your own home is always the best option.

Lorie Eber, JD, Gerontologist, CPT, Mayo Clinic Certified
Wellness Coach

You now have a comprehensive overview of all senior housing options. Choose a reputable company and thoroughly check out their credentials before placing yourself or a loved one in their hands.

Diane Mondini, President & Owner, Caring Companions At Home

Your Senior Housing Options

Diane Twohy Masson

Cover and illustrations by Steve Hartley.

ISBN: 1502898179
ISBN 13: 9781502898173

Library of Congress Control Number: 2014918870
CreateSpace Independent Publishing Platform,
North Charleston, South Carolina

Printed in the United States of America.

Dedicated to my mother, whose stories are peppered throughout. Being her advocate for over ten years has taught me to be a better person. My mom has dementia, but I am truly blessed that she still calls me by name. Her smile and joy inspires me to see the positive side of life. It makes me want to reach out and help seniors and their families make better choices today so they can have more secure long-term care plans tomorrow.

Special Thanks...

... to my family, in-laws, friends, colleagues, blog followers, seniors, and the Roll'n Hobos RV Group, who contributed ideas, stories, and inspiration.

This book would not have happened without my friend and editor Kim Kimmy. She and God kept nudging me to complete it. Thanks for never giving up on me.

To my trusted circle for final editing touches: my husband Chris, Jeannette Acheson, Stefan Moses, Joyce Ball, Marianne Casino, and Joan Reynolds.

To Jerry B. Jenkins for teaching me that less is more and advising me to shorten my original title.

To my savvy professional friends for their expertise: Joel Niblett, Kathy Kroll, Max Whiteman, and Craig Huish.

Thanks to the special few who offered testimonials : Steve Moran, Dr. Jim Gwinn, Lorie Eber, Joel Niblett, Craig Huish, Cathy Goodrich, John Styskal, Diane Mondini and Steve Fairfax.

My appreciation to the Alzheimer's Association for giving me permission to share dementia facts.

Contents

Contents

Contents

Foreword

As the publisher of a website about senior living, I was delighted to hear that Diane Twohy Masson was working on this book.

Curiously, most seniors fight the move to a senior living community because they fear losing everything precious to them. The truth is, almost every person who makes such a move wishes they'd done it earlier.

I appreciate Diane's comprehensive and realistic approach to evaluating senior living options, particularly her frank advice that you should not believe sales people 100 percent. Don't get me wrong. Most are honest, but her point was that seniors need to do their due diligence.

Senior living communities are the right option for many elders. This book should be read by anyone who wants a consumer friendly view of senior living.

Steve Moran, Publisher
Senior Housing Forum, www.seniorhousingforum.net

Introduction

Are you 65 years of age or older? One out of eight Americans are. This wave of seniors is called the silver tsunami. By 2030, the senior silver tsunami will have exploded to include one out of five Americans.[1]

Would you buy a lottery ticket if you had a 66 percent chance of winning? Two-thirds of seniors will need long-term care. Twenty percent will need it for more than five years. Women will need care for longer, for 3.7 years on average compared with 2.2 years for men.[2]

This book is your "how to" guide if you are a senior in the silver tsunami. Almost every adult can relate a horror story about a relative or friend who lived in a nursing home facility. It's usually an emotional story that breaks your heart when you hear it. I can still visualize my great aunt suffering in a nursing home bed and begging my mom to take her out of there. A few years later when I went to visit my grandmother at a different nursing home, I witnessed another resident trying to get away in a wheelchair. I watched as he was caught just beyond the grounds of the facility and his desperate escape attempt is forever etched in my memory. Some of my grandmother's

1 www.aoa.gov/Aging_Statistics/
2 www.longtermcare.gov/the-basics/how-much-care-will-you-need/

few possessions were stolen at that same facility. It left me with a permanent bad opinion of nursing homes.

Fast forward 25 years and I have seen wonderful skilled nursing homes with staff that provide loving care and treat the residents like gold. How do you find these homes? Well, you have to do your homework, look around, and compare facilities for yourself. This book will help you navigate the choppy waters of senior care to look beyond superficial issues to determine whether an independent, assisted living, skilled nursing care, memory care, group home, or Continuing Care Retirement Community (CCRC) would be the right fit for you.

You will have to make the pivotal decision of whether to move into a senior living community providing the appropriate level of care, or wait until a crisis develops. Here is my story.

When my mom was 73, we started exploring senior housing options. We searched for two years, visiting 20 retirement communities. My mom was lonely and hated eating alone. I knew she would love the social life of a retirement community. We saw some sad facilities, ate some horrible food, found a general lack of independence, and asked a lot of dumb questions.

My mom and I did not know what we were doing or what questions to ask. No one explained to us the difference between a rental community and a buy-in Continuing Care Retirement Community. My mom kept saying, "I don't want to live with all those old people." Her favorite question to ask was, "What percentage of the residents drive?" In most independent retirement communities few do.

After two years, we happened upon the perfect place and when my mom asked how many residents there drove the answer was, "Almost all of them." Hallelujah! It was a great place that we both loved. My mom put her home on the market, my sister and I held a huge moving sale, and two months later my mom moved into a Continuing Care Retirement Community.

Soon after, the marketing director at that community decided to leave and move to Minnesota. My mother-in-law encouraged me to apply for the position. I had never worked in senior housing before but had extensive experience in sales, marketing, advertising, events, and public relations. Four interviews later, I was working in the place where my mom was living. I already loved the place, so it was wonderful. That was 1999 and since then I have been a regional marketing director, corporate director of sales, and a consultant in senior housing for various senior living organizations in several states. It's my niche and I love it. The more I learned about senior housing, the more I realized how naïve I was when originally shopping for a retirement community with my mom.

My mom enjoyed the best years of her life living in the independent setting of a senior community. She was catered to all day every day. Someone else made her main meal of the day (she always raved about the food), washed the dirty dishes, and cleaned her apartment. That gave her free time to do her three favorite things: reading the morning paper at a local Starbucks, playing bingo (which included winning regularly), and enjoying live entertainment and performances.

What about you?

You may be trying to determine how to age in your own home or whether you should move to one of those retirement communities. Retirement communities come in all sizes, qualities, and prices with different licenses for the various kinds of care provided. Let me help guide you through those choices of staying home or how to select a retirement community that will fit your care needs and price range. I will give you tips to direct your search and intelligent questions to ask care providers. Maybe you are a vibrant independent senior or maybe you have recently had a health care crisis. Either way, this book can help you with the answers you need to conclude what your move or next steps might entail.

Dear senior,

I wish someone had shared with me and my mom the information I am about to share with you. It would have saved my family a lot of wasted energy, time, and frustration.

In this book I provide my insider tips and advice from working in senior housing and hearing thousands of stories. Dirty secrets will be exposed! My goal is to help you move quickly through a process that I walked through with my loved one. My teams and I have helped thousands of seniors move into senior housing options that were appropriate for their situation. After reading this book you may become one of the seniors who admits, "I wish that I had done this years ago."

I sincerely hope this information will be beneficial in your search for answers,

Diane Twohy Masson

E-mail: diane@Tips2Seniors.com
Website: www.Tips2Seniors.com
Blog: www.marketing2seniors.net/the-blog-for-seniors/
Follow Tips 2 Seniors on Facebook

Chapter 1
Is There an Ideal Time to Move into a Retirement Community?

The silver tsunami is currently washing over us with 35 million seniors 65 years and older. Are you one of them? This wave is expected to double in the next 25 years. Additionally, people 85 and older make up the fastest growing segment of the US population and Americans are now living to ripe old ages of 90 and 100 years old. By 2050, there could be nearly one million centenarians in the country.[3]

How do you determine if or when to move into a retirement community? Moving out of your home of 30, 40 or 50 years can be a daunting thought. Like many seniors, you probably don't even want to think about it and so choose to stay put.

Which of these two silver tsunami groups sound like you?

1. Those who plan ahead before a crisis happens.
2. Those who make a decision after a crisis occurs.

---

3 www.nia.nih.gov/about/living-long-well-21st-century-strategic-directions-research-aging/introduction

A crisis can be anything from a fall, a diagnosis of a progressive disease such as Parkinson's, diabetes, osteoarthritis, Alzheimer's, or cancer, to a stroke or serious heart condition. Let's be honest. Health conditions can deteriorate at any age, but the statistics are much worse for a senior.

One of the toughest stories that most of us have heard at least once is the one about a friend or neighbor who takes a tumble and can't get back up. A broken hip can prevent someone from reaching the phone or calling out for help. Even mild dementia will make the situation much worse.

Then there are the stories of seniors who have fallen and been found two or three days later. My own grandmother was one of those. A neighbor found my Nana one week after a bad fall. She was dehydrated and was rushed to the hospital. It was a miracle that she did not die. After 30 days in the hospital she had recovered enough to move into a nursing home. The hospital discharge planner sent her to a house of horrors where she spent the last year of her life. It was a terrible place where residents tried to escape and thievery was commonplace. It was not a nice place to visit, let alone live.

Questions to ask yourself: Do I want to plan ahead for long-term care before I become weak and frail? Do I want my spouse or children to "put me some place?" Every senior is one fall away from a crisis. I can be vibrant but accidentally trip and end up in a frail condition. Do I really want my son or daughter helping me with my bodily functions?

Is There an Ideal Time to Move into a Retirement Community?

Is your health deteriorating?

If you have been diagnosed with a progressive disease such as macular degeneration of the eyes, dementia, brain tumor, stroke, cancer, and so on, one of two things can happen:

1. You can get your affairs in order and prepare for someone to care for you when you no longer can.
2. You can go into denial.

Denial: "I'm not that bad!"

Guess how many times that I have heard denial from a senior or a loved one? Hint: it is over a thousand times. The senior is usually using a walker or can barely walk, cannot hear well, and often cannot see well. Their cars sometimes have dents and scrapes from minor accidents. They are in denial about their situation and ability to live well.

Recently, a senior couple attended a presentation I gave about options for senior housing. The woman fell asleep three times (trust me, I was not boring) and her husband had to hold her arm to keep her steady on her feet when they left. He proclaimed, "We aren't ready to move yet! She has a bad back, but she is not that bad. Our daughter comes once a week to do the house cleaning and friends from church bring us dinner every night. We are doing fine. Our biggest challenge is that she does not cook." This couple needs help. In case you did not notice, this is called denial! The husband does not realize that he and his wife have become a burden to family and church friends.

His wife is no longer independent. What if the husband fell and was hospitalized? Without his assistance she would not be able to take care of herself. Since neither of them cook or clean, they are both dependent on the kindness and time of others.

Loneliness and isolation

Loneliness is another debiliating challenge for seniors. Even married couples can be lonely, especially when one person is no longer able to undertake an activity that both once shared, such as going to see performing arts or sports, golfing, playing bridge, or attending church. If this has happened to you, a large part of your social life may be lost. Many seniors solve this problem by joining a senior center to fill up their social calendar. But, if you become unable to drive your social engagements will end. If you're living alone, the only plate you see at the dinner table is your own. Now you enter a time when you are dependent on neighbors and friends (who may be as frail as you) or a loved one (if you are lucky enough to have some living locally).

Some seniors become so lonely they call 911 on a regular basis. I have heard this from my firefighter son-in-law and many of my friends who are emergency responders. They can only feel sorry for anyone who is lonesome enough to make a fake emergency call so as to talk to another human being and get some attention.

Cooking for one or two can be a challenge and a chore

It's much easier to cook for a family of four or more than to cook for one or two people. Many widows and widowers have told me that it is disheartening to throw away half a head of lettuce when other people are going hungry. For people trying to eat healthily, a salad, entrée, vegetable, and starch to complete a meal requires a lot of preparation and leaves a sink full of dishes.

Sometimes it's easier for a frail senior to just have a TV dinner (a frozen meal) or eat cereal. Preparing a nutritious meal is just too much effort. But there is not much nutritional value in cereal or TV dinners. Not cooking can cause a senior's health to deteriorate rapidly. Other seniors struggle with chewing fresh vegetables because of aging teeth, and some lose their sense of smell, which affects their ability to taste food.

Some of you may say, "Hey Diane, I eat well! I don't eat TV dinners. I go out to eat." Well, dining out can often mean abnormally large portions, hidden fat, and salt, which can affect your health, especially diabetes or high blood pressure. In the documentary, "Super Size Me," a man ate nothing but McDonald's food for 30 days and it badly affected his health. Are you eating healthily?

Falling, memory issues, and driving challenges

Falling is very dangerous for a senior. If a 60-year-old breaks a hip, it may only take a couple of weeks to recover. If an 80-year-old breaks a hip, it could take four weeks or more to recover, especially if they don't have the will to improve by going regularly to rehab therapy.

Some seniors have emergency call pendants in case they fall. But what if you are not wearing it when you fall or your fall knocks you out and you can't call for help? One senior I know fell in front of her door and paramedics could not get in to help her. Does your daughter have to call you twice a day to make sure you are okay, or does a neighbor have to check that your lights or shades change twice a day? Such interventions can ensure that you don't lie injured on the floor for hours. Some seniors have screamed for hours to no avail because the next-door neighbor never heard them cry out. As I shared in the introduction, my own Nana was not discovered for one week after a fall.

How is your memory? Are you getting forgetful? Crossword puzzles and mind games can help to keep your mind sharp. But, spending time alone increases memory challenges. It is vital that you speak with a variety of people every single day, as any active adult does, although few realize it. We engage with people at the grocery store, library, health club, mall, restaurants, bank, senior centers or clubs, fast food drive-through windows, and so on. People who are working get even more of this social engagement. If the highlight of your day is checking the mail or your best friend is the weatherman on TV, you are not social. If you think that you don't want to be with a bunch of old people you don't know, and that is what it means to go into a retirement community, then keep reading. Humans are social creatures. When we spend too much time alone we start to wither and die.

Tips2Seniors.net

Memory issues can cause you to take your medications incorrectly.
Missing medication doses or taking too many can result in serious
health consequences. Just before my mom moved to assisted living
my husband Chris picked up all her medications to have them bubble
packed by a pharmacist. My mom handed Chris a paper bag with all
her meds loose in it (out of the bottles). She said, "Chris, I know this
looks bad, but I have taken all these meds for years and I know what
I am doing." Chris said, "OK," and believed her. On his drive home, he
realized how much her memory had declined and how horrible the bag
story was going to sound to me. It turned out that some of those meds
she knew so well in that bag had expired.

We got my mom to assisted living—in the nick of time—and she immediately improved. Her health had been rapidly going downhill primarily because she was mismanaging her medications. I found it frightening that my mom was convinced that she was taking her medications correctly but hadn't been.

It was just another little fender bender. Poor eyesight, slower reaction time leading to a delay in hitting the brake, and early dementia leading to disorientation can result in accidents. Cars mean many different things to people. To a senior, they represent one thing: independence. That was the case for my mom. She drove to Starbucks every single day and even became a "Customer of the Month" there. People who witnessed her driving commented that she could not see over the top of the steering wheel.

My friend Brian's mom, Dorothy, who lives in Minneapolis, was cut off from church and daily swimming when she could not pass the driver's license exam. If you are going to rely on rides from family and neighbors, or public transportation, usually only the essentials get addressed. A neighbor might be willing to take you to the doctor or to get groceries but not for a daily swim or to your weekly card game. No car means isolation and isolation can lead to memory loss and memory loss can lead to...well you get the idea. It's a slippery slope.

If you can still drive well and safely, the world is your oyster! Enjoy your life and don't worry. Other seniors may think they are driving safely, yet when I speak to their adult children they have a different opinion. Please stop driving if you are jeopardizing yourself and others on the road.

Is There an Ideal Time to Move into a Retirement Community?

Are the day-to-day basics too much for you?

- Have cooking, personal grooming and cleaning your home become overwhelming?
- Is it too much effort to get daily exercise?
- How is your dental hygiene?
- Do you still see your dentist once or twice a year for check ups and cleanings?
- Can you still care for your pet? Does your dog long for a real walk?

- Are your toenails so long that they are reminiscent of Howard Hughes?
- What about upkeep of your fingernails and cuticles?
- Have you changed your hairstyle so you don't have to go to a stylist as often?

Conclusion: It's all about choices

If you have a history of falling, forgetfulness or if you suddenly have a fender bender or two, it is time to make a plan, and soon. It is better to have a plan than to wait for another crisis. We all like to make our own choices. Make your choices now. Seniors can get so frail that suddenly they can't make their own choices and a family member, attorney, or a close friend may have to make decisions for them. Do you really want someone else making your choices for you?

Some seniors start sleeping in the recliner because it is too much trouble or too painful to manage the stairs and go to the bedroom. Have the day-to-day basics become too much for you? When everything becomes a struggle, you may have actually lost out on the opportunity for independent retirement living and have to look for assisted living.

The next chapters will compare home care options with moving to a retirement community.

Chapter 2
"I Want to Stay in My Own Home."

Staying at home is always an option. Change is very hard for anyone but particularly for seniors. Many senior men have said to me, "Diane, they are going to have to take me out of my home feet first." Do you know what this means? Another phrase to use would be "taken out of the home horizontally" or on a stretcher—not a pretty picture.

Costs and responsibilities of home maintenance and upkeep can be more than you realize. Let's take a look at your lifestyle and costs if you choose to stay in your home and age in place.

Senior homeowners with a paid-off mortgage still have:

1. Property taxes—which tend to increase
2. Home insurance
3. Roof and window repairs
4. Painting of the exterior every five to 10 years or the high expense of re-siding the exterior
5. Garage/carport maintenance
6. Exterior porch/deck/steps maintenance
7. Gutter cleaning

8. Furnace maintenance and cost of fuel (gas, oil, propane)
9. Air conditioning maintenance
10. Electrical maintenance
11. Yard/garden maintenance
12. Interior maintenance—painting/plumbing/electrical
13. Window washing—exterior/interior
14. Exterminator for big bugs, spiders, ants and pest maintenance
15. Snow removal (unless you live in a warm climate)
16. Utilities: Electricity, gas, water, sewer, garbage
17. Cable TV
18. Internet
19. Landline, cell phone, or both
20. Housekeeping (this cost can be eliminated if you can do it yourself)

Senior homeowners have a lot of bills, upkeep, and constant maintenance to preserve their investment in their homes. Even with a paid-off mortgage, monthly costs can increase over time. This list does not include groceries, other necessities, medications, health insurance, car maintenance, and gasoline.

- Condo owners have homeowner association dues that handle much of the exterior maintenance. These dues can dramatically increase or you can be assessed for a high dollar amount at any time.
- Mobile homeowners are in a similar situation as householders but with additional costs to rent their park spots.
- Renters are also in a similar situation as householders for items 13 through 20 with rental insurance instead of homeowner insurance.

Mowing the grass and gardening

Most seniors agree that hiring yard work helpers does not provide the same quality as doing it themselves. It is very hard for avid gardeners to wait another week for the gardener to come and pull the weeds, trim the bushes, and mow the grass. Homeowners lose control when someone else is performing the work, and they may have to supervise the help at every little task to ensure the results reach their standards.

The price of a clean home

Are you still performing housekeeping to the same quality that you once did? Is changing the sheets too much for your back? Are you letting cleanliness standards slide bit by bit? Do your children express concern about the condition of your home? Do you find yourself deciding not to invite people over because you don't feel like cleaning? Cleanliness is important for your health. Maybe it's time to ask for help by hiring others to do the work or asking a family member or your local church to support your cleaning efforts.

Depending on children, neighbors, or a loved one

Isn't life ironic sometimes? Babies are dependent on parents for every physical and emotional need they have. Did you change your children's diapers and attend to their every need for years? Your responsibilities may have included feeding, bathing, and transporting them to school, doctor appointments, and ball games. Is turn around fair play at this point in your life?

When you can no longer drive safely, is it your child's responsibility to take you to doctor appointments, the grocery store, or to pick up the pharmacy prescriptions? The next step would be having your child cooking for you and cleaning your home. The final step would be having them change your diapers, feed, and bathe you. Most parents do not want to go down this final path.

Some parents are more than willing to live with their children. Unfortunately, in this situation, everyone loses privacy. Yet I have also witnessed the trade-off blessing of having three generations living together. The little ones love having the grandparent in their home and vice versa. Some grandparents can babysit their grandchildren until the parents get home, saving money on childcare. Aging parents living with adult children can be a beautiful thing and many caregiver children say it was the greatest gift they could have given their parents in their final years. They are grateful for quality time spent together. But most caregiver children have said it was hard to become the parent and have the parent become the child.

Maybe you never had children or they became estranged over the years. In those situations, who do you turn to when you need help? How much can you really ask of a neighbor? I have heard of situations where an entire neighborhood comes together to support one senior. The neighbors take turns bringing dinner, getting groceries, and taking the senior to the doctor.

I have also had desperate neighbors come to my retirement community and say, "The adult children have no idea that their mom needs help. My neighbor, Gladys, is not OK. I am getting completely worn out trying to help her. I have my own family to take care of, and they feel neglected." When that same neighbor brought Gladys to take a tour of the retirement community, it was disconcerting to learn that Gladys was oblivious to the burden she had become for her neighbor. "I am fine in my home," she said. "My neighbors look in on me."

Setting up a Power of Attorney (POA) for finances and health

Regardless of if or when you will move, it's never too early to make a plan for who will advocate on your behalf if you are suddenly not able to communicate your own wishes. Most seniors pick their spouse, one of their adult children, or a close friend.

Set up your Power of Attorney (POA) for finances. This paperwork needs to be handled by an attorney. Hopefully, you have a family member whom you trust. You can appoint him or her for this key role. Otherwise, you may need to pay a professional such as an attorney to handle your finances when you become incapacitated through an accident or through the natural aging process.

Set up your Power of Attorney (POA) for health care. This document is very important for anyone having surgery, because there is always a chance that person may not wake up and the POA would direct that person's health wishes.

My husband and I each have POA for my mom. We can make decisions jointly or independently. Only one of us needs to be present to make a decision regarding my mom. This works for us. I will never forget the time my mom was in the hospital after a fall. I informed the doctor that we wanted no tests that would require her being sedated, as sedation could permanently intensify her dementia. The doctor seemed to agree. However, the next thing I knew, my mom was not in her hospital room and we learned that she was being prepped for a test that required anesthesia. We had to race down two floors to stop them and got there in the nick of time. Afterward, the doctor apologized. Ultimately, the person you select to have POA has to be willing to be a vigilant advocate. What if I had not been nearby and available to come to the hospital to intervene?

Plan ahead before a crisis—or you may bypass independent living

If you or your spouse have a new health diagnosis or are getting frail, what might happen?

Many seniors don't realize that senior living communities often have minimum health requirements. If you have a diagnosis of a progressive disease, you may not qualify for certain types of housing. If you are in the later stages of Alzheimer's, you may only qualify for memory care or skilled nursing care.

It is illegal for a senior housing care provider to let you move in and not be able to provide for your needs. Many seniors are stunned when they arrive at an independent senior living community to be told they have bypassed an independent living setting and that an assisted living community would provide a more appropriate level of care for them.

"I Want to Stay in My Own Home."

The conversation that a retirement counselor in a senior housing community dreads most is "the talk" with a future resident. As I write this, one Continuing Care Retirement Community (CCRC) that I work with had to turn down two applicants in the last six weeks. One applicant had a diagnosis of dementia and could not manage alone, and the other was too frail for independent living. Even though those seniors thought they were fine to move into independent living, they only qualified for assisted living. Other CCRCs I worked with in the past would deny people admittance if they had *ever* had cancer, Parkinson's, Alzheimer's, multiple sclerosis, or anything that would send them quickly into a higher level of care for an extended period of time. How can they do this, you might ask? Well, it is a contract for services, and as long as they are consistent with all applicants, this is considered consistent with fair housing practices.

Senior housing? Not me—not yet!

Does this sound like you? "I don't want to live in an old folks home with a bunch of old people I don't know. It would be a nightmare hearing about their aches and pains." This is a very common sentiment. You don't relate to every neighbor in your own neighborhood and choose to spend time with those who are like-minded and have similar interests. Read chapter 8, "What is the Lifestyle Really Like?"

Maybe you are not a good candidate for senior housing and home care might be a better option for you. Study the chapters in this book and then do your due diligence.

Caution: Do not select a senior community based on price or on one person's opinion. Dig deeper to determine the organization's financial stability, care reputation and staff turnover.

Tips2Seniors.net

Consequences of waiting too long

When you can no longer care for yourself, you must depend on your children, friends, and neighbors. Any caring person is more than willing to help in an emergency, but who will provide long-term help? Many seniors burn their bridges and become a burden to those they care about the most. A friendly neighbor or loving family member can burn out providing daily support for a needy senior.

Now add isolation and increased memory loss to your problems. These also increase vulnerability, so one apparently kind person can come and take advantage of you and steal your money. So beware and be very careful! Elder abuse is widespread!

Are you living on your credit cards?

Do you live beyond your means every month? Are credit cards paying for the upkeep of your home? Did you put the last home repair on a credit card? Seniors can become mired in credit card debt. If you live beyond your means every month, it will catch up with you.

My friend Alice has consistently outspent her income by $900 every month for the past several years, and now she has $50,000 in credit card debt. Alice's monthly repayments are wreaking financial havoc on her and will do so for the rest of her life. Whether you are carrying one or several credit card balances, it can come back to haunt you. Credit card companies require a payment each month and charge you significant interest. Dementia can affect the timeliness of your future payments and cause you to rack up penalties. This in turn can create a spiral effect of bouncing checks as your monthly costs continue to escalate.

Make every effort to create a repayment action plan the first month you can't pay off every penny on your credit card.

Reverse Mortgages

 Tip: Be careful of hidden costs and long-term ramifications.

My mom considered a reverse mortgage at the age of 73. She could no longer afford escalating home maintenance costs. Mom was only considering this as a short-term solution. Thank goodness she had me look over the paperwork so I could explain the long-term impact of a reverse mortgage. She would have lost control of her biggest asset. If she had needed to suddenly move to a higher level of care, the reverse loan would have come due and she would have had limited choices. A reverse mortgage can provide short-term monthly cash, but the hidden costs and compound interest can quickly eat up your eligible loan amount. The bank then owns your home and you no longer have that asset to use for future health care needs. What would you do?

Reverse mortages can be helpful in certain cirmcumstances, but it is an irreversible choice. Be careful and request expert help.

Conclusion

The cost of staying in your own home is higher than many seniors ever imagined. Paying property taxes, painting every five to 10 years, and replacing a roof every 15 years are huge expenses. So take the time to calculate all expenditures on a monthly basis. That nice senior living community down the street may not be as expensive as it first sounded. Living in your own home and bringing in care may not be your least expensive option.

Beware: Some seniors use credit cards or reverse mortgages to pay for home maintenance and chore services, which may increase their debts to the point that they become too much to manage. My mom was eventually unable to afford to live in her own home. This is now happening to a good friend of mine who is 85 years old. Her assets equal her credit card debt. Please consider the long-term financial consequences of your decisions.

If maintenance and upkeep of your home have become a burden, it may be easier and more affordable to move to a retirement community where it's all done for you, removing one more source of stress from you and your family.

It is vital to make power of attorney arrangements for finances and health. Do all your end of life paperwork. It is a responsible gift to give your spouse and children if you have them.

Ultimately, if you refuse to move from your home, you can become a burden to your family and neighbors. With age, you can become more frail and weak. Your family member can worry about you, then a crisis happens, and they are forced to "put you someplace."

Chapter 3
The Facts on Home Care

What is home care? It is having a paid caregiver come into your home and do chore services for you. They cannot legally provide nursing services or dispense medications. Here are some examples of what a caregiver *can* do:

- Provide companionship;
- Cook one or all of your meals;
- Clean your home;
- Run errands, such as grocery shopping, taking you for a haircut, picking up your medications or other necessities;
- Drive you to the doctor or dentist;
- Provide stand-by shower assistance;
- Help you to get dressed;
- Do laundry and ironing; sew on buttons.

Home care costs

Most nonmedical home care companies have a minimum hourly cost, usually starting with a requirement of approximately four hours of care per day. Costs can run $18 to $25 or more per hour. The national average hourly rate for home care was $20 an hour in 2012.[4] The more

---

4 www.metlife.com/mmi/research/2012-market-survey-long-term-care-costs.html#keyfindings

expensive companies tend to have better reputations, and let's be honest, you get what you pay for.

Most home care companies require a four-hour minimum. If you need caregivers both morning and evening, then you will normally be charged for eight hours. This can become very expensive very quickly.

At the time of this writing, reputable around the clock nonmedical home care can cost somewhere in the vicinity of $15,000 to $18,000 a month, not including nursing care.

Beware: Typically, home care companies do not provide daily oversight to determine the quality of care provided by the caregiver. For example, caregivers working for home care companies are not legally required to record whether a senior did or did not take his or her medications. Most families don't realize this, and it can be dangerous for a senior's health to rely on nonmedical caregivers.

Short-term or long-term caregivers

Caregivers are very handy when you have just arrived home and are recuperating from a hospital stay, a recent surgery, or a rehab stay.

They can be your temporary hands and feet when you may be confined to a chair or bed. A caregiver can get your groceries, cook, do dishes, laundry, walk the dog, empty the litter box, and anything else that is too hard for you to do.

 Tip: Prepare a list of tasks so that you get value for your money.

Couples may use a caregiver on a long-term basis when one spouse needs assistance and the other does not. Your husband or wife may need stand-by shower assistance a couple of times a week. Most couples in this situation use a caregiver about two or three times a week with a four-hour minimum per day. It gives the well spouse a break. This is a good alternative, enabling a couple to remain together in the home.

 **Tip: At some point the caregiving will have to increase from two or three days a week to around the clock. Can you afford it? Are you willing to give up all your privacy? Moving to a community that offers the support you need could cost one-third the amount of around the clock home care.**

Hiring a home care company

Before you select a home care company, do your due diligence and make sure it is a reputable company with longevity. Ask for and check references. Check online for reviews. Talk to both the seniors receiving the care and to their adult children who are typically managing the caregivers. Often the senior sees their caregivers in one light and the adult children regard the caregivers in quite another. Remember, most of us never like to admit that we made a mistake. The advantage with hiring a home care company (as compared to "a nice lady from church") is that you may be able to select from several caregivers whose case manager or supervisor provides weekly spot checks to determine quality of care.

 **Tip: Don't just ask a reference if he or she is happy with the caregiving service—ask specifically what they like best and least.**

Hiring your caregiver "under the table"

You may save significant money by hiring a companion recommended at church or your neighbor's friend who has been out of work. It's a win-win for everybody—right? Wrong! What is your recourse if something goes wrong? There is no boss or company to whom you can voice concerns.

Caution: At the 2014 Care Revolution Conference in Anaheim, California, I met over 20 home care company owners and managers. One manager told me that most of her caregiver applicants do not pass a drug test. I was shocked. Another told me that nearly half of the remaining applicants don't pass the criminal background check. Reputable agencies have a vetting process that screens out these applicants so seniors can have some confidence about who is in their homes providing care.

Double caution: Reputable home care company owners also informed me that seniors who hire a caregiver "under the table" effectively become employers and are responsible for taxes and Social Security of their employee. Check with your accountant and consider the ramifications of paying quarterly taxes for an employee. Initially, it may sound like a bargain to pay a caregiver "under the table." Please consider the long-term financial consequences.

Triple caution: If your "under the table" caregiver submits a claim for an injury sustained while working for you, costs can climb up to $300,000 after surgery, therapies, and time lost from work. Some caregivers work for multiple companies, so you never really know if the injury was from working for you or another employer.

My friend's dad lives in Pennsylvania and has four part-time caregivers working for him. Two work during the week, and two work on the weekends. They have scheduled days and loosely designated hours. For example, they may work two to four hours each, depending on what needs to be done. Then they go to him and say, "Don, I have worked three hours. I made you breakfast, changed your sheets, did a load of laundry, and cleaned the kitchen." Then Don pays them for three hours of work. He has to do this with each caregiver twice a day, every day.

Here are some of Don's recent comments to a long-distance child: "Lola thinks she is the boss of me. She's going through my clothes and things. I think she drank one of my diet colas. She watches me when I eat. Now she is asking for a raise, and I said no. I will be out of money in one and a half years."

When Don's caregivers want a day off, he has to simply agree and not have anyone for that shift. Recently the caregivers have started arguing among themselves. Don has to referee and finds it wearying. Each says the others are not doing their jobs. Every day, Don needs to manage and pay the caregivers. This is a lot of work and added stress for an older man who is not fully independent. He also needs one of them to take him to the bank regularly, so he has cash to pay them. This entire situation could blow up for this family if anyone of the four caregivers started to steal from or abuse Don in any way.

One of Don's long-distance children checks in on him about once a month. Another has given up every Saturday and Sunday evening with his own family for years to make Don's dinner. When this does not happen, Don, age 94, heads for a fast food restaurant. Guess how he gets there? Let me put it this way. I would not want to be on the road when Don is driving. He thinks that he is doing great.

Managing your caregiver

You are paying for a home care company to provide you with a regularly scheduled caregiver. The caregiver needs to show up on time and provide the care or companionship that you need. Some seniors don't realize they have to manage and potentially feed their caregivers. Caregivers have issues too—they get sick, have family obligations, and need vacations.

Sometimes the caregiver and senior click and become friends. Relationships between others can be as unpleasant as fingernails on a chalkboard. Both personalities and communication styles need to be compatible. For example, my mom does not hear well, so caregivers need to speak loudly. Other things to consider are: Does the caregiver have a gentle touch? Is he or she lazy, loud, or abrasive? Does he or she smoke? Does he or she do a mediocre job of cleaning the home or just sit and watch TV? Is he or she kind to your animals? Do you feel safe and secure when your caregiver is home with you?

What happens if your caregiver doesn't show up?

If the caregiver doesn't show up, a family member will need to come to your rescue, if one lives nearby. If you don't have adult children or children who live locally, then you need a backup plan. What if you are relying on caregivers to pick up your medications or to take you to a crucial doctor appointment?

> **Beware:** I have heard of several situations when a senior was stuck on the toilet because no one was there to provide assistance.

Firing a caregiver or company

The Internet and other media are filled with stories of elder abuse such as the one I recently read about a son who had to fire three caregivers for not providing adequate care for his parents. Just as this son learned the hard way, families don't realize how much supervision is required. Some caregivers are absolutely wonderful and other steal from and abuse their clients.

A senior shared a story with one of my colleagues. "A caregiver stole $300,000 worth of my jewelry and family heirlooms." The jewelry had been given to her by her mother and grandmother and was irreplaceable. Her family fired that caregiver, but they never got any of the items back. They went on to hire a new caregiver they all love.

If you hired the nice lady from church, then you must deal with whatever comes from firing a person who knows all your personal information and could exploit you. She may have hungry mouths to feed and it can be devastating for all concerned. On the other hand, if you hired a home care company and a caregiver is lazy or not working out, then a simple phone call to a manager can bring a new replacement the next day.

Live-in caregivers

Sometimes you can get a caregiver to live with you. At first, it sounds ideal because it costs less (even with room and board) compared to the $15,000 to $18,000 a month you would pay a reputable company for around the clock home care. But by doing this, first, you lose your privacy and second, you leave yourself open to being taken advantage of financially. Live-in caregivers can go through your things while you are sleeping and ultimately control your whole life. You are at their mercy.

> **Beware:** Please be very careful. I have heard from adult children who have witnessed abuse of their parent, have read numerous stories of such abuse in the newspaper, and have seen it happen to one of my neighbors whose caregivers confined her in her own home and took over her finances.

Medication management? No!

Nonmedical caregivers cannot dispense medications. They are considered personal attendants and can only advise a client when it is time to take his or her medications. If you are looking for good oversight and medication management, then move to a community with fully licensed personnel who offer exactly that kind of care.

Home care and dementia

Home care and dementia are not a good mix. Seniors with dementia are vulnerable. This is not a good time to put yourself in a paid employee's hands. Do you have a son or daughter that can oversee your home care on a daily basis?

Tip: If you are depending on a caregiver to dispense medications, think again. Even if your caregiver is a certified nursing assistant, they can only legally dispense medications in a licenensed community under the direction of a nurse. Home care caregivers are simply paid companions who can do chores. Most have not been medically trained.

If both you and your spouse have dementia, then home care may not be a good solution for you. My in-laws are in this situation. Since they both have dementia, neither can be responsible for allocating the proper medications several times a day. But remember, home caregivers are paid companions, not paid medically trained personnel who will document medications received.

Regulations governing home care

Home care regulations vary from state to state. Be sure to check them out in your state.

For example, in California, no special home care business license is required. Owners of reputable home care agencies are appalled that fly-by-night home care companies can start up without fingerprinting employees, checking criminal backgrounds, or even providing good training. Any home care agency in California can hire staff and put them to work in a senior's home the next day with no training. Unbelievable!!! Please be careful.

On the other hand, some states, such as Washington, have more regulated home care. One requirement is that a caregiver completes a specified amount of training before working with a senior.

Tip: Licensing to operate a nonmedical home care company varies from state to state. Find out if caregivers are required to be minimally trained in your state. Learn if drug screening and criminal background checks are mandated or voluntary. Legislation is constantly changing, so check your state's regulations.

"How do I pay for nonmedical home care?"

The national average pay for nonmedical home care increased by 5.3 percent from $19 an hour in 2011 to $20 an hour in 2012.[5]

There are a variety of sources that may help you pay for home care or supplement your private pay funds. Here are a few that you can explore.

- Commercial insurance
- Long-term care insurance

_____

5 www.metlife.com/mmi/research/2012-market-survey-long-term-care-costs. html#keyfindings

- Medicaid waivers
- A Medicaid state plan
- Older American's Act (OAA) Title B Supportive Services;
- Title III E Family Caregiver funds
- Veterans benefits (contact your local VA Hospital).

Home health care

Home health care is a step up from home care. Think of it as providing medical care at home, such as a nurse or therapist coming to your home rather than going to an office to receive care. Because the practitioners are more highly trained, the hourly fee is higher than for home care and varies across the country. When a senior is discharged from a hospital, insurance may pay for home health care, but usually only for a short time, depending on the situation. If you are able to stay at home rather than in a hospital or skilled nursing facility it can cost your insurance company less money.

Most people only use home health care professionals on a short-term basis. Long-term home health care provided by a certified professional is very expensive.

Medicare Part A (Hospital Insurance) and Medicare Part B (Medical Insurance) covers eligible home health services such as intermittent skilled nursing care and physical therapy, among others. A home health care agency can coordinate services ordered for you by your doctor. However, Medicare will not pay for 24-hour care at home or for personal nonmedical care.[6]

---

6 www.medicare.gov/coverage/home-health-services.html#1367

Sources for home health care funding include Medicare, Medicaid, the Older American's Act, the Veterans Administration, and private insurance.

Conclusion

Home care can be an ideal way to get temporary care when you are recovering from a hospital stay. It can be a godsend for an elderly couple to stay together in their home. But providing long-term home care is a challenge. The cost is prohibitive for most seniors and can rapidly deplete their savings. Around the clock home care can cost two or three times as much as assisted living or skilled nursing care.

Remember this: If you need medication management at home, home care will not provide it; it only brings nonmedical companions to your home.

In reality, a caregiver is a paid friend. If you have any type of dementia, how will you manage this caregiver? If you have no children, or if your children live far away from you, do you have a back up plan if a caregiver fails to show up?

Make sure you select a reputable company and that you only need companion-type services. Know what you are paying for and be prepared to manage your new employee. Have a plan in place to fire that employee if he or she is not a good fit, abuses you in any way, or steals from you. If you need intermittent nursing care at home, then contract a home health agency that can provide a certified professional.

Check with your accountant about the tax implications of hiring a caregiver "under the table," as by doing so you become an employer. A senior in need of help might not be able to become an employer and pay quarterly employee taxes.

If you are likely to need home care over the long-term, calculate the annual costs. For how many years will you be able to afford a full-time caregiver? Don't wake up one morning with no options. Plan ahead.

Keep reading the next chapter to determine if a senior housing option may be a more affordable option for long-term care. Each option has health and financial implications, so plan ahead.

Chapter 4
Senior Housing Options and Costs

"At least 70 percent of people over 65 will need long-term care services and support at some point. **'Medicare and most health insurance plans, including Medicare Supplement Insurance (Medigap) policies, don't pay for this type of care, sometimes called 'custodial care.'** Long-term care can be provided at home, in the community, in an assisted living facility, or in a nursing home. It's important to start planning for long-term care now to maintain your independence and to make sure you get the care you may need, in the setting you want, in the future."[7]

This is a quote from the official *Medicare and You 2014 Handbook*, page 63.

Searching for senior housing options

Those caught up in the silver tsunami can find senior living options through a variety of sources. Here are some common primary resources:

- Reading this book (congratulations, see how responsible you are being already!);

---

7 www.medicare.gov/Pubs/pdf/10050.pdf

- Internet searches;
- Word of mouth at social engagements, parties, and church;
- From friends who experienced senior housing options in crisis mode;
- Visiting those friends while they were in crisis;
- Volunteering at a local nursing home;
- Inquiring with your doctor or pastor for suggestions;
- Driving by a local retirement community and stopping in to tour;
- Asking your senior friends for recommendations;
- Recommendations from an adult child or family member;
- Receiving a direct mail piece from a senior living community;
- Invitations to events at retirement communities;
- Newspaper advertisements for events or free lunches to explore a senior housing option;
- Realtors;
- Attorneys;
- Investment advisors;
- The local phone book.

 **Tip: You can conduct secondary research by following a retirement community on social media, such as Facebook, to learn more about the lifestyle there.**

Online resources

Surf the web to explore senior housing or care level options online. Just type in the keywords of the type of housing you are looking for, along with your city and state, into the search bar. Here are some examples:

- Independent retirement living, "my city and state";
- Continuing Care Retirement Communities, "my city and state";
- Assisted living, "my city and state";
- Memory care, "my city and state";
- Skilled nursing care, "my city and state."

Online referral sources can help direct you to possible housing choices with an online menu or an advisor. This service is provided for free to you. But, please be advised that some will only direct you to a senior living provider who has either paid or contracted to be listed with them. Many of these online referral sources also have great articles or blogs that provide more information on senior living. Here are some examples:

- Caring.com;
- Aplaceformom.com;
- Iseniorsolutions.com;
- Ourparents.com;
- Seniorhomes.com;
- Seniorliving.com.

Independent living

 Stand-alone independent living retirement communities typically offer rental apartments or some other month-to-month contract. Apartments can vary from studios to two-bedroom apartments to stand-alone homes. Independent living retirement communities typically provide:

- One or more meals per day;
- Social activities;

- Outings and trips on the retirement community's bus;
- Transportation within a certain radius for medical and dental appointments;
- Maintenance of the apartment and community spaces;
- Utilities, except phone.

Other services such as housekeeping, linens, personal laundry and an emergency call system may or may not be provided.

They can provide wonderful options for socialization and it is comforting to know that people are around—you are no longer alone. Hopefully, the food is fantastic.

 **Tip: If you are not happy at a rental retirement community don't stay there. Move out and find a retirement community that you do like. They are not all the same.**

Two downsides of an independent living rental community:

1. Eventually running out of your financial resources and being kicked out the next month.
2. You will eventually require a higher level of care than many rental communities can provide.

Some independent living communities also have assisted living options. That usually means that most people in the community need assisted living services and a few people are independent. This is not a good option for a vibrant senior who is likely to be miserable there. When assisted living services are needed, the monthly fee will go up considerably.

Key question: Ask how many current residents use assisted living services and how many are independent.

Many independent living communities cannot legally provide any routine care to their residents. So they may partner with a home care agency that can provide personal care services for their residents. Each resident can contract with the home care company. In this case you and your loved ones will still need to manage the caregivers, including firing them if necessary. In this situation, you have your monthly cost of living in the community and the additional expense of caregivers.

Key question: Ask what percentage of residents use caregivers; this will give you a good idea how many are truly independent.

Independent living costs

Costs for independent living communities vary widely across the country, from $800 for lower income models with no services, to $8,000 a month for a three-bedroom apartment in a new community. Average costs are typically $2,000 to $5,000 a month. Always ask what services are provided. Comparison choices are usually not apples to apples.

Key questions: Find out what the annual cost increases will be. You should ask to see the past five years of monthly fees, which will show the increases. Increases of over 5 percent usually means that the community is paying off considerable debt (such as the mortgage of the community with interest payments). Ask what their debt is. In my experience, average debt is around $50 - $100 million dollars for a retirement community. The higher the debt, the more likely it is that your monthly fee will increase dramatically in the future.

More key questions to understand the facts about independent living retirement communities

- What is included in the monthly cost? Get very specific.
- What are the extra costs?
- If you run out of resources, what happens to you?
- When you need more care, who provides it?
- Do they provide medication management? How much does this cost?
- What happens if there is an emergency and you go to the hospital?
- Who answers the emergency call system?
- Do they have a nurse on site? If yes, what services are provided, for example, blood pressure checks. Nurses can be limited by the retirement community's license, so a nurse at one retirement community may provide different services from a nurse at another retirement community down the street.
- Do they provide transportation to the airport? Does this cost extra and if so how much?
- Where do you wash your personal laundry? Is it located in your own apartment or down the hall in a community laundry?
- Always ask, "What should I be asking that I have not asked yet?"
- Ask a lot of questions! Ask for clarification if you don't understand.

Assisted living

An assisted living community essentially provides independent living with added support. It could be that you just need help with medication management, dressing, cueing (prompting) to meals, or a stand-by shower assist. This is called helping with one or more of the "activities of daily living" or ADLS. Residents in assisted living communities typically have a private room and bath (though the shower may be down the hall).

Another term for an assisted living is a board and care. These are usually regulated by the state and have surveys to evaluate qualtity of care as often as every 12 months to 60 months. Here is an online tool to research your state's information: http://www.aplaceformom.com/ assisted-living-state-licensing.

Assisted living social model compared to the medical model

The difference between a social model and a medical model is the amount of time a nurse* is on staff each week at the assisted living community. A senior with Type 1 diabetes may need an insulin shot three times a day and a nurse on staff for more than eight hours a day to check your blood sugar levels and manage your medication. In this case you would need a medical model assisted living. In a social model, a nurse will typically be available for about forty hours a week and will not be able to accommodate a senior with Type 1 diabetes. If you opt for a social model, you might have to pay extra for outside help, if it is allowed in the community. Carefully research which model will work for your current and future health needs.

*Tip: Ask what type of licensed nurses work at the community, a registered nurse (RN) or licensed practical/vocational nurse (LPN/LVN)? Ask how many hours the nurses work per day and whether there is a nurse on duty around the clock. Be very specific. RNs are the most qualified to serve the higher acuity needs you will need as you age and need more care.

Stand-alone assisted living retirement communities are typically offered on a rental basis or another term is month-to-month contract. They typically provide:

- Three meals per day, plus snacks;
- Social activities;
- Outings and trips on the retirement community's bus, depending on residents' acuity and physical abilities;
- Transportation within a certain radius for medical and dental appointments;
- Maintenance of the apartment and community spaces;
- Utilities, except the phone;
- Housekeeping one time per week;
- Linen service as needed;
- Care for residents with cognitive impairments;
- Caregivers 24-7;
- A nurse 40 plus hours a week;
- Incontinence care (this almost always costs extra);
- An emergency call system.

Most importantly assisted living communities are regulated by the state. Their staff document:

1. Medications given to residents;
2. Any change in the resident's condition;
3. Any new physician's orders.

In my experience, most residents in assisted living need help with medication management. Find out who oversees and dispenses the proper medications, because it may differ by community and state. Ask questions! It's helpful to have a nurse on-site at least 40 hours a week to assess if you might need to go to the doctor. If you fall in the night, someone should find you within hours. For a frail senior with no children nearby, this is a great option. The quality of care does vary and cheaper does not mean just as good. You get what you pay for.

 **Tip: Look around and evaluate the cleanliness of the community. Find out how often they do a deep clean, such as moving furniture and cleaning underneath the bed.**

My mom lived in assisted living for seven years while she progressed from light dementia to full blown vascular dementia. In the early years, she socialized with the more alert residents and by the end of her stay she ate with other residents with similar cognitive issues. My mom was at the highest care level that could be provided at her social model assisted living. Her needs in the last few months included:

- Medication management three times per day;
- Assistance with dressing (buttoning buttons, for example);
- Stand-by shower assistance two times per week;
- Around the clock incontinence care;
- Cueing for all meals and activities;
- Reminders to safely use her walker;
- Nurse checks on her feet once a week, because of her Type 2 diabetes.

For the last year that my mom lived in assisted living I lived a 1,000 miles away from her. It was comforting to know that she was taken care of socially and physically. In certain circumstances, it can be very difficult to make care choices using a power of attorney (POA) without being there in person. POAs are covered in chapter 2, "I Want to Stay in My Own Home." When my mom's health suddenly changed, I hired a geriatric care manager to assess my mom, escort her to the doctor, and be my eyes and ears. In a two-week period of time, I made the dramatic choice to move my mom to a skilled nursing community near me.

Costs and point systems

The cost of assisted living varies dramatically. Most communities have a base rate and add on costs for all care services. The base rate covers room and board (meals) for an independent person who needs some support. The care needs will determine extra costs that are either charged on a care level system, point system, or an all-inclusive pricing program.

The base rate does *not* typically include:

- Cueing to meals;
- Stand-by shower assistance (one or two per week);

- Completely dressing the resident;
- Personal grooming;
- Incontinence care;
- Medication management;
- Additional companion services.

Tip: Care can cost more. Find out how much more. The community either prices care services individually or you receive a maximum package of care at each care level.

Key questions: What will be the total cost of my daily care? As I age in place, what is the maximum cost of care? At what point would I be asked to leave the community because of my care needs? Where would I go?

Beware: Some assisted living communities promise you a low base rate and will determine the care costs based on your needs after you move in. This is often a gimmick. They hope that you will move in and not want to leave even if the added care costs are higher than your budget. Get the full costs and compare them with all-inclusive rate communities. Initially all-inclusive rate communities may sound like a higher cost but could save you thousands in the long run.

By law, an assisted living community must provide you with a written disclosure of the care they provide. It is against the law for them to admit someone and not be able to provide for their care needs.

Nationally, the average cost per month in an assisted living community was $3,427 in 2013.[8] Base costs can range from $2,200 to $6,000 per month depending on where you live and how new the community is. Extra care options can cost anywhere from $300 to $6,000 a month. Some assisted living communities can legally provide more extensive care if you are willing to pay for it.

The Aid and Attendance Program/VA benefits can help pay for assisted living.

If you are a veteran or a spouse of a veteran, then you may qualify for VA benefits, which could be worth around $1,000 or $2,000 a month. You must meet certain financial and health requirements to qualify—beware of independent retirement communities that say you may qualify for this benefit. A certain level of care is required to access VA benefits, usually two or more activities of daily living provided by a community or caregiver.

Beware: Some financial advisors charge seniors $500 to $800 to prepare the paperwork to qualify for Veterans Benefits. This is supposed to be a free service.

---

8 www.johnhancock.com/about/news_details.php?fn=jul3013-text&yr=2013

Author's personal note: I would personally like to thank you if you or your spouse has served our country.

Residential board and care homes/adult family homes

Residential board and care homes, also known as adult family homes, are usually small homes for four to six residents in a residential neighborhood. One live-in caregiver typically provides the care. Do your homework before you choose one of these. Some are similar to assisted living models while others provide higher levels of care that compare with skilled nursing care. They are known by a variety of names in different states.

The quality of care provided varies dramatically. Some of these homes are owned and run by nurses while others hire a live-in caregiver. Usually one caregiver provides the care, cooks the meals, bathes and toilets the residents, cleans the rooms and home, creates activities and converses with the residents. It is an incredible amount of work for one person. I have heard the most wonderful heartwarming stories of love and care provided in such homes, but I have also heard nightmares of neglect. Be diligent in checking references to find a good quality residential board and care home.

This setting, though, may not offer an active senior enough stimulation. A larger assisted living community with a wider array of social opportunities and outings may be a better fit. However, frailer seniors may benefit from the individual care that a residential board and care home can offer.

In some states, licensing for residential board and care homes can fall under the same state regulations as larger assisted living communities.

Ask to see the home's current license and latest survey (some states call it a Facility Evaluation Report) and clarify any areas of concern. An online search for "licensing for elder care" along with the name of your state should lead you to licensing regulations for your state.[9]

Tip: Good residential board and care homes usually stay full and have wait lists. Don't wait too long to get on the list, as they may not have an opening for one to two years by which time you may be ready for the care they provide.

Prices vary dramatically by state and care provided. According to "A Place For Mom," typical pricing is $3,500 to $4,500 a month. Homes specializing in dementia care can cost from $5,000 to $6,000 per month.

Tip: Some adult family homes may cost less than the averages listed above, depending on location and whether or not it is a family-run business.

Additional funding sources include long-term care insurance and Medicaid. Some adult family homes do not accept Medicaid, while others may require you to pay privately for one or two years before utilizing Medicaid.

The advantage with an adult family home is that it provides a more home-like environment. The disadvantage is that there is often only one caregiver on site.

---

9 Special thanks to Karry's Eldercare in Laguna Hills, California, for this great tip!

Key questions: Check to find out who supervises the caregiver and what their duties are. Is there a second caregiver scheduled during the day? Is the one and only caregiver really awake in the middle of night? Talk with the caregiver. Does he or she look tired, stressed, or harried? Find out if the caregiver lives in or works in shifts with others. Is there an RN on site at all times? If not, how often is an RN on site? Are residents just reminded to take medications or are the medications administered? Interview and tour four or five homes before you choose one.

Memory care

According to the Alzheimer's Association over five million Americans live with Alzheimer's, two-thirds of whom are women. One in three seniors die with Alzheimer's or another form of dementia.

Memory care communities can be stand-alone or incorporated into an assisted living or a Continuing Care Retirement Community. The staff has been trained to work with residents with Alzheimer's and other types of dementia. Some communities are licensed as residential board and care facilities (such as assisted living) and others are licensed under skilled nursing.

There are four stages of memory loss. In the first two stages, the sufferer can live in an independent living setting and move to assisted living as the illness progresses. Stages three to four can vary widely in impact on the patient but most people can be accommodated in an assisted living or skilled care nursing.

Stand-alone memory care communities are usually secured, so that residents cannot wander away and get lost. Sometimes they are called locked communities. Others may have a wander prevention alert system, which sounds an alarm if a resident is near or goes out an exit door. Staff can then quickly redirect wandering residents back into a secure area.

Dementia is not considered a disease but a symptom of a disease that showcases memory decline. This cognitive decline affects the ability to perform everyday activities. Alzheimer's disease accounts for 60 to 80 percent of those affected with dementia.[10] The second most common type of dementia is vascular dementia, which my mother has and slowly progressed until she could no longer take care of herself. Fortunately, she has never been a wanderer.

People with Alzheimer's disease forget the current year, then the last five years, and so on. It is horribly sad to see a person who can no longer recognize his or her own children or spouse. Many come to believe that their caregivers are their parents.

A word about mystery shopping: If you are not familiar with this term, it it an undercover evaluation of a senior living community. It can be performed by an individual or a company that specializes in this. Senior living communities may hire a mystery shopping company to evaluate the presentations and effectiveness of their individual employees.

In mystery shopping memory care, I have encountered facilities with up to 30 rooms for residents. The rooms typically surround one large community space where the residents eat, socialize, and participate in

---

10 www.alz.org

activities. It's nice when memory impaired residents have the freedom to access an outdoor area to walk and get fresh air. Check for yourself: several communities I visited in one state locked these outside doors so residents would not get sunburned in summer or frostbitten in winter.

Some of the most caring staff that I have ever known work in memory care settings. There can be touching moments to witness such as when a woman with dementia rocked her baby (a doll) to sleep. Her husband told me that she had never been able to conceive and had multiple miscarriages many years before. That heartache was gone for her now, as her new reality was rocking her baby. An angry man with dementia can suddenly become calm when he is handed the tools from his former profession, such as giving a plastic tool belt to a carpenter.

So again, do your homework. The quality of memory care communities varies widely. Visit four or five communities. Remember that a secure memory care facility may not be required if the patient does not wander.

Memory care costs

Secured memory care communities can typically cost $5,000 to $8,000 or more per month, depending on location and the age of the community.

Skilled nursing care

Skilled nursing care provides nursing care, 24-hours a day, seven days a week. It can be needed for a short-term stay after a surgery or for the long term in cases of debilitating illness. Generally speaking, skilled nursing facilities are subject to surprise surveys by the state; the Center for Medicare and Medicaid Services (CMS) determines if they can remain Medicare and/or Medicaid providers.[11] Typically, a resident in a skilled nursing care facility shares a room with one other resident, though many still have three-bed rooms. Private rooms cost more. Smaller skilled nursing communities can have twenty beds; larger ones have up to 500 or more.

You can ask for the results of the facility's last survey to determine any areas of concern. Survey concerns should have been addressed but remain on the record until the next survey. Staffing should always be at or above the level required by law.

In my experience, the best looking communities do not always have the best reputation for care. Do your homework and check out four or five communities. Care is the most important consideration, along with the quality of the food and management.

 Tip: Skilled nursing care is a high staff turnover business. What is the staff turnover rate of the community you are considering?

Key questions: What is the longevity of staff? Look for administrators, directors of nursing, and management staff who have been working in the industry for several years. Make sure most management staff have been at the community for one or more years. If the administrator has been there for less than a year, ask how long he or she has been working

---

11 www.cms.gov/Medicare/Provider-Enrollment-and-Certification/CertificationandComplianc/
NHs.html

in the industry. Shy away from a community with short-term or inexperienced management staff.

 Tip: What do you feel when you walk in the door? Go with your gut. Visit at least four or more communities and you will immediately recognize differences.

Skilled nursing care costs

The average yearly cost for a semiprivate nursing home room with skilled nursing care, nationally, was $82,855 a year in 2013. The average for a private room was $94,170.[12]

For a short-term stay, skilled nursing communities can work with a variety of insurance companies including Medicare. Depending upon your supplemental insurance coverage and qualifications, a stay of one hundred days or fewer could be paid in full.

For a long-term stay, a senior could drain his or her savings account or assets paying for skilled nursing care. Medicaid insurance, a government program for low-income seniors, will pay most of the costs of skilled nursing care if you qualify. Most skilled nursing communities accept Medicaid. But, what no one knows is how long the government will be able to fund it. Don't depend on it. As baby boomers age and people live longer the pressure on Medicaid will increase.

My mom qualified for Medi-Cal in California, which is similar to Medicaid, but the paperwork needed to apply is overwhelming. My mom receives

---

12 www.johnhancock.com/about/news_details.php?fn=jul3013-text&yr=2013

Social Security income, a small pension, and an annuity that took a major hit in 2008. Her depleted savings account held only $2,000. After a rigorous qualification process, Medi-Cal examined her assets and income and determined the total cost that my mom is responsible for every month. Medi-Cal pays the balance, which includes a visiting medical doctor, dentist, optometrist, and most of her other medical needs. She pays for all her personal needs such as laundry, haircuts, and so on.

Senior Housing Options and Costs

Continuing Care Retirement Communities (CCRCs)

A CCRC typically provides three levels of care on the same campus. They usually include independent living, assisted living, and skilled nursing care. Some have memory care on site, which would be a fourth level of care.

Apartment sizes in these communities range from studios to custom 2,000-plus square foot penthouses, casitas, villas, or cottages.

As you age, you move through these levels of care. With a CCRC you and your family know what quality of care and settings to expect in the future and you will not have to find a new place to live when you need a higher level of care. CCRCs can be a godsend in the case of a sudden health change.

Continuing Care Retirement Community (CCRC) lifestyle

The lifestyle in these communities can include nice details such as multiple dining venues, cocktail lounges, quality entertainment, lifelong learning seminars, saline swimming pools, golf simulators, state-of-the-art exercise equipment, hiking clubs, spas, and woodshops.

The typical CCRC lifestyle includes:

- Live entertainment (check their schedule to see what they provide and how often);
- Exercise programs (yoga, tai chi, and strength training);
- Line dancing and karaoke;

- Card games (bridge, poker, and hand and foot);
- Trips and cultural outings (this varies widely);
- Billiards and Wii bowling;
- Swimming;
- Putting tournaments;
- Art studio (some are active and others stand empty);
- One to three meals a day;
- Housekeeping (once a week or once a month);
- Maintenance of the apartment and grounds;
- Transportation to medical and dental appointments;
- Educational and wellness programs;
- Salon and barber services;
- Health care on site including
  - Wellness Clinic in independent living settings (not all offer this);
  - Assisted living;
  - Skilled nursing care (some places call themselves a CCRC and do not offer this key level of care);
  - Memory care (not all CCRCs offer this).

CCRC residents have the security that future health care needs will be addressed on the same campus. Most CCRCs can handle almost any health concern with the exception of those that require hospitals or mental institutions.

How do you access healthcare in a Continuing Care Retirement Community (CCRC)

Assisted living at a CCRC is a planned move. This decision usually includes you, your doctor, your family, and the community. Check the contract before you move in to see how this decision is made at the community you are considering. Single seniors with no family find comfort that a CCRC can help transition them to the next level of care during a health care change or crisis.

Ideally, but rarely, a couple will move to assisted living together. The rooms are usually smaller, so that a couple can share a small one-bedroom apartment or live in two side-by-side studios.

In my experience, one member of a couple becomes frail or gets dementia first and can live on in the home with support from a spouse for a while. As long as the needy spouse can toilet, bathe, and dress him or herself, the healthy partner can manage the medication. At a CCRC, someone else will cook your main meal of the day, clean your apartment on a regular basis, and drive you to medical appointments. Other professionals on-site will take care of your feet and do your hair (some of these services cost extra). For a couple with one declining spouse, the healthy spouse can still socialize daily with other residents and staff to maintain his or her own sanity and intellect. If you don't use your brain on a regular basis, you will suffer cognitive decline.

When one spouse can no longer completely care for the other in the apartment, caregivers can be hired for a few hours a day. Depending on how a CCRC licenses their buildings, home care may be provided by qualified staff in the independent setting or a resident may hire home care caregivers from an outside agency. If that becomes too burdensome, then you can make the decision to move your spouse to a higher level of care or move to assisted living together. No one ever moves willingly to skilled nursing care together and it is rare to have a couple in skilled nursing together.

Couples want to be together forever, but two people's health will not usually decline at the exact same rate. Your doctor may prescribe skilled nursing care after a hospital stay and suddenly one spouse is living alone in independent living while the other is in skilled nursing care. At a CCRC, a spouse can typically walk to visit the other in nursing care.

Tip: Look for a CCRC that provides multiple care options on the same campus before you get to the point of needing care or support.

Double tip: Some CCRC's are in urban settings and residents can walk to local restaurants and shops. Others are in more rural settings and residents must rely on the CCRC transportation when they can no longer drive. Decide which you prefer.

Continuing Care Retirement Community (CCRC) costs

Most CCRCs require a one-time investment and monthly fees. The one-time investments vary widely from $60,000 for a studio in some areas of the country to about two million dollars for a brand new penthouse. Monthly fees can range from $1,000 to $6,000 a month depending on size, services provided, newness of the community, and the entrance fee you select. The average monthly cost varies from $2,000 to $4,000 a month for one person. The monthly fee for a second person is normally $600 to $1,500 a month. CCRCs in metropolitan cities with views will cost the most while a CCRC in a more rural setting or a smaller town will be much less.

Caution: Seniors typically sell their home in order to pay the CCRC one-time investment. It's always a good idea to have a deposit on your apartment of choice before you put your home on the market. I have had desperate seniors, whose home sold quickly, want to move into an apartment with a specific floor plan and none was available. A second move within the community added stress simply because they failed to plan ahead.

Tip: It's always best to have a deposit on an apartment before you list your home.

Key question: The monthly fees increase annually, so check the CCRC's five-year history on increases. A consistent annual increase of over 5 percent indicates considerable debt. Debt-free CCRCs are rare but provide more financial stability for the residents.

Tip: To determine if a CCRC is financially stable ask if it has been certified or accredited by a third party. Accreditations by third parties cost a company time, money, and resources. A former CCRC where I worked went through this internal examination and on-site survey process. It took months. Go to www.carf.org for more detailed information on their ongoing requirements.

Key question: A portion of the entrance fee may be returnable to you or your family, after you leave the community vertically or horizontally. Consider your family and estate needs before you choose a CCRC. Do you want to leave an estate to your children or spend every dime before you go? If you have no children and want to leave your money to charity, consider your options carefully. Of course, none of us knows how long we will live, but if you have no serious illness and come from a long-lived family, you could live for many more years. You may need a guarantee of care. Keep reading for more information on that topic.

Entrance fee/one-time investment

What does the one-time investment (entrance fee) cover? It allows for a lower monthly fee in independent living for life (compared to a higher monthly rent in a rental community) and may also cover discounts for higher levels of care. Many CCRCs have plans that can be similar to long-term care insurance. Some CCRCs give a 25 percent discount for life in assisted living or skilled nursing care, compared to the public rate. Many CCRCs accept nonresident patients into their assisted living or skilled nursing care facilities. Other CCRCs are considered closed campuses and do not allow the public in their assisted living or skilled nursing care.

Five typical variations in returnable entrance fees at Continuing Care Retirement Communities (CCRCs)

- Non-refundable fee or a fee amortized over a time period to zero percent returnable—this is typically your most economical choice.
- Fifty percent returnable—a fee amortized down to a minimum of 50 percent returned to your estate, costs more than the non-refundable fee.
- Seventy-five percent returnable—a fee amortized down to a minimum of 75 percent returnable, costs more than the first two options.
- Ninety to 95 percent returnable—these are the highest priced entrance fees but obviously the highest returnable rate to you or your estate.
- One hundred percent returnable—typically only brand new communities in development offer this because they need 70 percent of the building reserved in order to build.

Tip: It's easier for seniors to sell a home in order to pay this one-time investment than to sell stocks or draw from a 401K account.

The amount of the entrance fee returned to you or your estate will depend on the rate of depreciation outlined in the contract and the time you spend in the community. Entrance fee amortization typically occurs over two to five years. Some families go so far as to create spreadsheets to determine the best option based on a senior's current age, health issues, monthly income, and total assets. This is a very individual choice and one that only you can make to suit you and your family needs.

Tip: It might be possible to write off a portion of the entrance fee on your tax form for the year that you move in. Talk to the CCRC staff about this and ask what type of paperwork they would provide your accountant. Check with your tax advisor to see if this benefit is available to you. You may also be able to write off a portion of the monthly fee. This can be a great tax benefit if you itemize your deductions.

Double tip: Some CCRCs allow short-term payment plans for the entrance fee if you have your home on the market to sell.

Guarantee of care for life

Very few CCRCs offer a guarantee of care for life. Those that do can make up the difference of your monthly fee in independent living, assisted living, or skilled nursing care if your resources are depleted through no fault of your own. Make sure this benefit is included in the contract, if it is offered.

"Through no fault of your own" means that you cannot give your money away to children or a charity and then have the community take care of all your financial needs.

Tip: Read the contract carefully and do not rely on the verbal promises of the sales representatives.

Continuing Care Retirement Community (CCRC) contracts

There are three types of CCRC contracts, Type A, Type B, and Type C, as generally described here.

- Type A CCRCs are the least common. They are life care communities and their contract costs more than other types. Residents pay the same monthly fee as they progress through independent living, assisted living, and skilled nursing care. The predictable fees for all levels of care can create security for people who prefer to plan ahead. The financial burden falls on the community if extended care is needed.
- Type B CCRCs are the most common. They have modified contracts and cost less than a life care contract. Some allow for a return of the entrance fee when you move to a higher level of care. Others give 25 percent discounts for higher levels of care or offer free days of higher care. The burden tends to fall equally on communities and residents for future health care costs.
- Type C CCRCs are fee-for-service organizations charging market rates at all levels of care. These are also known as a rental contract and offer no discounts for higher levels of care. The

burden for future health care cost falls directly on the resident and the community carries no long-term risk.

Tip: Read the fine print in the contract. Find out what would happen if you ran out of money. Ask when your family would receive the returnable portion of the entrance fee and whether that would be returned regardless of whether you are alive or dead when you leave.

Double tip: Check with your state for governing parameters and definitions of CCRCs (for example, one of the requirements in the state of California necessitates life care communities to provide a guarantee of healthcare coverage for life with no exceptions).

Hospice care

Hospice care can begin when a doctor has determined that someone is near death or is terminally ill with six months or less to live. A hospice support team brings comfort care to both a senior and his or her family members, either at home or in a senior living community. Ask the independent retirement community you are considering if it is allowed. Hospice care may require a senior to have continual around the clock help from a caregiver or family member.

It's common for hospice support to work with assisted living, memory care, and skilled care nursing communities. Since these communities offer around-the-clock care, it relieves family members from the need to be with the hospice resident at all times. The goal should be to have the most homelike setting possible.

Tip: The health of the senior often determines the proper hospice setting. Skilled nursing communities can better handle higher acuity care residents, so research what is best for you or your loved one.

Health requirements for any level of care

Many seniors and their family members don't realize that the various retirement communities, including independent living, assisted living, skilled nursing, and Continuing Care Retirement Communities, all have health requirements for new residents. Physician orders are required for a higher level of care. All the communities I have worked with require a current doctor's report signed by your doctor (paid for by you) as well as an in-person interview assessment conducted by the community's nurse or administrator.

Tip: Many people wait too long to find a retirement community and find they no longer qualify for independent living or CCRC settings. Seniors typically want to wait until right before a crisis is likely and then move into a community, but no one has a crystal ball to know when that crisis will happen. Choices made in a hurry are not always the best.

Emergency call system question for all levels of care

An emergency call system can save lives if it includes medically trained staff who *immediately* respond to the call.

Key question: Who answers your emergency call system during the day and in the middle of the night? Some places only have a receptionist or security guard available to answer the call.

 **Tip: It's always best when a medically trained person answers the call light, such as a nurse or emergency medical technician. Making sure such personnel are available, before you move in could save your life. Be a detective and ask questions.**

Traveling for all levels of care

Do you still love to travel? How close is the community you are considering to the nearest metropolitan airport? Can transportation take you to meet a 6:00 a.m. flight, or will you use the airport shuttle?

 **Tip: Consider how easy or hard it will be for your family to visit. Where will they stay? Are there guest apartments and how readily available are they? How much do they cost?**

Conclusion: Good News and Bad News

Plan ahead so you can make your own choices and not have someone "put you some place" when you are incapacitated. Many good communities are full and have wait lists. The smart thing to do is to get on the wait list for your community of choice and wait for your perfect apartment or cottage to become available. Otherwise, you may have the extra burden of moving twice within the same building to get the view or floor plan that suits your lifestyle.

Here is a summary of the advantages and disadvantages of the various types of retirement communities.

- Independent living communities do not require a buy-in (plus side), but if you outlive your resources you will be kicked out (negative side). When you need a higher level of care, your family will have to find a new assisted living or skilled nursing community for you (negative side).
- Stand-alone assisted living communities vary widely on how much care they provide. Most important is how many hours of the day a nurse is on duty. They are regulated by the state and medications are documented. Plus, when you need a higher level of care, your family will have to find a skilled nursing community for you in a crisis.
- Residential board and care homes have a homey setting (plus side), but the quality is only as good as the one caregiver can provide (could be negative).

- Memory care communities are usually secured for wandering residents (plus side), but most are small and the quality varies widely (could be negative).
- Skilled nursing care is never anything that someone chooses. It can be for short- or long-term stays. Base your choice on care first and not what the community looks like. Some places that are not pleasing to the eye provide great care.
- Continuing Care Retirement Communities (CCRCs) may initially seem the most expensive. In the long term, they can offer discounts for multiple care options after a hospital stay. Do the long-term math; many are similar to long-term care insurance. A CCRC could be your least expensive option, especially if part of the entrance fee can be returned to your estate.

Please do your homework when selecting your senior housing options. Visit four or five communities within several days, so you can easily recognize quality differences. Keep reading for more tips and advice.

Chapter 5
The Seven Deadly Sins
of Searching for Senior
Housing Options

1. **Being desperate and needing housing immediately**

   - Your house sold more quickly than you anticipated.
   - It's just too hard to manage on your own.
   - Your doctor just diagnosed you with dementia, Alzheimer's, congestive heart failure, or some other disease.
   - You are in the hospital and will need further care when you are discharged.
   - Your adult children say that it's not safe for you to live alone.
   - The car is sporting another new scrape.
   - Your doctor recommends that you move to assisted living soon.

If you wait until crisis mode, good luck! You will get what you get and it may not be what you need or want. It's much better to research your options while you are fully functioning and able to drive and get around. Most seniors want to wait until right before a crisis happens to move. Well, no one knows when that crisis will happen, so it's impossible to plan a move for immediately before it happens. The older we get, the more likely it is that a fall or some health diagnosis can change our life in a millisecond.

For example, if a senior is in the hospital, the discharge planner usually gives the family 24 to 48 hours to select a nursing home. This is not a lot of time, particularly when your family wants to spend time with you while you are hospitalized. If your family is living a distance from you, this is even more challenging.

My father-in-law asked me and my husband to select a nursing home for my mother-in-law after she fell and had a bout of pneumonia. What if we had not been available? I was already familiar with the reputation of the local nursing homes (since I am in the business and lived in the same area) and was quite shocked at what our mystery shopping uncovered. One salesperson ignored the screaming lady that we walked by, as if she did not exist. My thoughts? Next, please! In the second place we visited, when I asked about sharing the bathroom, they said they put every resident in diapers. We headed rapidly to a third place where they didn't seem to care. But the fourth place was vibrant and wonderful. It was an extra 20-minute drive for my father-in-law but it was worth it.

 **Tip: Please don't just take the advice of the discharge planner, without checking it out for yourself. Once you're in a skilled nursing care facility it can be very difficult to change to a new one should you be displeased.**

A dirty secret exposed: Kickbacks are illegal, but in some small towns, they are given and received. Some doctors only recommend one facility of which they are a partial owner. You would be very surprised!

2. Basing your decision solely on price

Everyone wants a good deal, but in my experience, cheaper does not mean quality in senior housing. You get what you pay for. Less expensive communities have to cut costs somewhere and it is usually in staffing.

Staffing is the biggest cost in any facility. Night-time staff levels can be very important in assisted living or skilled nursing care communities, particularly if you just pushed your call light because you have to go to the bathroom. The second biggest cost is food. When one of my friends was recovering from a hernia operation, he stayed at a rehab center that ran out of food for one meal. They almost always ran out of the protein item on the menu and one morning when he asked for a second pancake at breakfast he was told there were no more.

Senior living communities have set expenses. Staffing, food, and utilities are the biggest expenses. In order to cut costs, staffing or food will be cut. It is a lot to ask an overworked small staff to cook, clean, and care for the residents.

Another dirty secret exposed: Less expensive retirement communities typically serve cheaper cuts of meat. Each chef is given a budget to cook breakfast, lunch, and dinner. I have witnessed angry and upset chefs vent about mediocre budgets. Study the menu to determine how often the residents get protein. Salmon with chardonnay sauce, baby back ribs, and filet mignon may never be served at lower-priced communities, even on special occasions.

Caution: Some retirement communities will assess fees (for such things as property tax) after you move in. Find out *specifically* what is included or excluded in the price.

3. Not planning for long-term costs

If you are considering selling your house, you may have the maximum financial nest egg when you make the initial move from your home.

Consider the tax consequences of selling your home and the possibility that you might owe capital gains tax. Many seniors will not have any tax to pay from the sale of their residence. This is because the US Tax Code allows each taxpayer to have an untaxed gain of up to $250,000 on their home sale ($500,000 tax free gain for a couple). If you have some after-sale cash from the sale of your home, you could use some of that money to pay toward an entrance fee at a Continuing Care Retirement Community.[13] I am not a tax

---

13   Craig Huish, CPA, Waterfront CPA Group

advisor, so check with yours on what may be the best choice for your situation.

Tip: Cashing in your IRA or stocks can bump you into a higher tax bracket. Get advice and develop a financial strategy to choose which assets to use for future care. Remember that skilled nursing care can cost $82,000 a year. If you bring an around-the-clock caregiver or home health professional into your home, it can cost even more.

At first glance, most seniors want to spend as little as possible each month for health care. Rather than paying the large upfront fee to buy into a community, some seniors want to hang onto their money and make monthly payments in a rental facility. It's important to consider the long-term costs and consequences of all these choices.

Another dirty secret exposed: Believe it or not, some people don't realize that you can get kicked out of a rental community if you don't have enough money to pay your monthly rent. Many seniors think that because they are elderly and have lived there a long time, they will be allowed to stay.

Seniors rarely think about the fact that they could live in a rental community for many years and run out of the assets that supplemented the monthly income to pay the rent. This puts them back in crisis mode. A buy-in Continuing Care Retirement Community may cost less in the long run and offer more for your money. Do your homework and research your options. Study chapter 6, "Key Facts on Rental Communities Versus Continuing Care Buy-ins."

Key question: Factor in the additional cost of the yearly increase at the senior living community. You have a right to ask for a five-year history of monthly increases. Beware of communities with annual increases over 5 percent. While operating costs do rise yearly, a well-managed community will also manage their budgets properly. A year-over-year increase of more than 5 percent in monthly fees can indicate considerable long-term debt at the community. Ask about each community's mortgage debt. The community generates revenue from the monthly fees to pay for their mortgage debt and ongoing operational expenses.

4. **Judging a community only by appearance, apartment size, or location**

It is tough to move out of your 2,000-plus square foot home into an apartment.

Tip: It's a mistake to decide where you will live based on apartment size alone. You must evaluate the entire community.

Some senior living communities look great but will provide less than optimal care in the long run.

Adult children often want their parent to move into a retirement community just down the road from them. Don't base your decision only on location, number of bedrooms, or apartment size. Diligently compare all aspects of the geographically desirable community with its competitors farther away.

Tip: The easiest way to compare differences in quality is to visit several communities over a short period, such as a few days or a week.

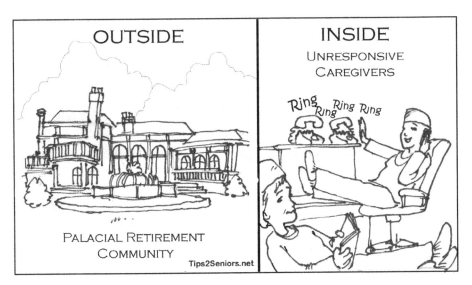

5. **Not asking the right questions**

Before I knew much about this subject and was merely a daughter helping a mom, neither my mom nor I had any idea what questions to ask about a retirement community. As I have already said, my mom's favorite question was, "How many people here drive?" This was a great way to find out how many residents were truly independent.

Here are five intelligent questions to ask:

- **Does the retirement community have a mortgage?** It is important to know about the community's debt. In my experience, the average senior living community has from 50 to 100 million dollars worth of debt. A community I worked at in Portland, Oregon, had 225 million dollars worth of debt and one in Seattle had 250 million dollars worth of debt. The amount of their debt will be a determining factor in whether or not annual costs will get out of control and is a huge factor in determining how much the monthly fee increases year over year.

- **How are the apartments, cottages, or villas, priced?** Some are simply priced on size. Other communities charge more for apartments on the first floor or the top floor. Various communities will have a different price for each apartment, based on size, floor plan, and view. If you don't ask specific questions about price, sale representatives may steer you to an available apartment. But if, for example, you know the first floor costs more, you might want to wait until a less expensive second floor apartment comes available.

- **How long has the majority of staff worked there?** There is a lot of staff turnover in the senior housing business. I have heard of communities that are missing their executive director, bookkeeper, activity director, and marketing director all at the same time for several months on end. This is not unusual, but it is terrible for residents. Most staff members are only at a community for around one year. This is not good. Look for staff longevity, especially in management as they train the rest of the staff.

- **Ask about the experience of the administrator.** If you ask this question at a random sample of four senior living communities, three out of four administrators will probably have worked at their community for less than a year. Ask a second question about how long the administrator has been licensed and worked in this industry. The longer their tenure and experience, the better.

- **Do they offer a guarantee of care for the rest of your life?** A few Continuing Care Retirement Communities (CCRCs) put this guarantee in writing (this is the best situation). Quite a few imply it through the sales team. Always ask to see the contract. Rental communities with a month-to-month contract will just kick you out when you can no longer make the monthly payments. So, be careful. My mom ran through her assets in seven years of assisted living. This can happen to seniors receiving higher levels of care. There is more in-depth information on this topic in chapter 6, "Key Facts on Rental Communities Versus Continuing Care Buy-ins."

6. **Believing the salesperson 100 percent**

Let's face it, some salespeople are just great and can sell cooking lessons to Betty Crocker. Study the fine print on the contract. Does the agreement for services reflect what the salesperson just told you? If there is a legal dispute, your only recourse will be to fall back on the written contract.

7. **Avoiding asking a friend or relative to help you evaluate your choices**

Please ask someone to provide another set of (objective) eyes help to evaluate your final two choices. Let them experience interactions between staff and residents. Listen intently to their reactions and carefully watch their facial expressions and body language. Don't let your opinions influence them beforehand.

Caution: Let's be honest, some adult children only think selfishly about their inheritance.

Double caution: Some financial planners do not consider *your* best housing option; they are more concerned about decreases in their monthly or yearly commission.

Some people don't want to involve their adult children or friends in this decision, because they want to maintain their privacy or don't want to inconvenience others. It's your life and your money, but be sure to do all the proper due diligence in evaluating your choices.

Here is an analogy that may help you: Think back to when you or your friend's teenager was considering what college to attend. Would it have been responsible to visit only one college? That would not have been wise. It was a big life decision. So is this. Enlist help and look at several places.

Conclusion

Smart seniors plan ahead and research their options. Don't get caught in a crisis. Once you are in crisis mode, your options may be very limited. These seven deadly sins are a summation of my work with thousands of seniors during the course of my career.

The seven deadly sins of searching for senior housing options.

- Being desperate and needing housing immediately
- Basing your decision solely on price
- Not planning for long-term costs
- Judging a community only by appearance, apartment size, or location
- Not asking the right questions
- Believing the salesperson 100 percent
- Avoiding asking a friend or relative to help you evaluate your choices

Chapter 6
Key Facts on Rental Communities Versus Continuing Care Buy-ins

Many people ask me what the differences are between rental communities and Continuing Care Retirement Communities (CCRCs) with a buy-in fee.

In answer to this, there are several key questions for you to ponder through this chapter.

Many retirement communities decrease the frequency of services included in their monthly fee to make it sound more affordable, then add the individual costs back in. Suddenly, your average monthly cost may be more at what you thought was the lower priced community.

> **Caution:** I just learned of a CCRC that took the cost of electricity out of their monthly fee so they could compete with another CCRC a few miles away. Unwary seniors may be fooled into thinking these two communities have similar monthly fees but one now has an additional monthly fee for electricity and cable TV that could run to several hundred dollars.

 **Tip:** Seniors generally look at costs first, but you must compare apples to apples. Please do a thorough investigation before you jump into an agreement based on looks or price alone. For example, property taxes may not be included in the monthly fee but could be a yearly cost assessed on each apartment.

Calculate long term cost differences

Most people tend to look at cost differences first. Who wants to lay out a large one-time investment if it is not necessary? Paying month-to-month may seem like a better way to go. That's what my mom thought. Then I did the math, looking at the total cost difference between the rental community and the CCRC that she was considering over a period of years.

For the rental community, I took the monthly fee and multiplied it by 12 months and then multiplied it by four, five, six and seven years. (Technically, I forgot to add in the yearly increases.)

For the CCRC, I did the same as above and added in the one-time investment, which was not eligible for return to her or her estate after five years.

The break-even point was year six. If my mom lived independently for six years, her cost per month would start to drop at the CCRC compared to the rental.

Hint: This breakeven point will be different for everyone based on location, the initial investment, and the amount of that investment that can be returned to the estate.

That one-time investment was a stumbling block for my mom until I broke it down for her and she finally understood the full costs of each community. We considered her age and health and gambled that she would live for six more years. Ultimately, the benefits provided by the CCRC were similar to the benefits that would have been provided by a long-term care insurance policy if she had purchased one, as the one-time investment in the CCRC included benefits for assisted living and skilled nursing care.

The gamble paid off, because she lived in independent living for eight years before transitioning to assisted living on the same campus for seven more years. In the middle of those seven years, she ran out of resources—she did not have enough money to pay her monthly bill. Her Social Security, small pension, annuity, and savings account had dwindled to $2,000.

The CCRC had a Good Samaritan Fund (explained below) and so she did not get kicked out—the CCRC made up the difference from the fund. It was, amazing, incredible, and an answer to my prayers. Had my mom made the right decision 15 years earlier? Yes, she had and as a result enjoyed great quality of care for all those years in assisted living.

Tip: If my mom had chosen the rental retirement community, she would have been kicked out when she ran out of money to pay her monthly payment. Lesson learned: It pays to do your homework and research all the costs.

Risk of future health care costs: on you or the community

Another way to look at selecting a rental versus CCRC is to consider the future health care costs as a risk factor.

A rental community takes on none of this risk, leaving it all to you. You pay as you go on a month-to-month contract. If you can't pay or they can't provide the care you need, you must move. (Sadly, this can happen in the middle of a health care crisis.)

Current news: National news outlets are carrying a story (2014) about a 103-year-old who is getting kicked out of her rental community. The community had doctor testimonials to prove they could not provide the care she needed. This grandma is to be evicted from her home.

Contrast rentals with a CCRC that considers your age, health, and finances before you move in. They are gambling that you will not need a higher level of care for an extended period of time. For this reason, many CCRCs will not accept someone in the later stages of a disease requiring a high level of care.

Tip: The best time to select a CCRC is before you have any major health challenges. The older you are when you apply for a CCRC, the less time they will need to take care of you, but the greater your chances of needing health care.

Many senior communities use actuarial studies, which look at the projected life expectancy of a senior man or woman. Life expectancy continues to lengthen with modern medicine, but the average person lives to be about eighty years old. I know a resident of a retirement community who will turn 100 this year. She is a spunky firecracker who enjoys a daily swim and a glass of wine. Some states foster greater longevity. Statistically, residents of California live longer than residents

A few Continuing Care Retirement Communities (CCRCs) offer a guarantee of care. This is a gray area, so ask lots of questions and look at the contract to see exactly what they offer.

- Some CCRCs offer a Good Samaritan Fund for residents who outlive their resources. This is not a guarantee. It means that they have a fund. Find out the criteria and process to receive funds. Ask how it is replenished and what happens if multiple residents need it at the same time, or if it becomes depleted.
- Some CCRC contracts include a guarantee of care but with a scary caveat: "At our option." Find out *exactly* what this means. Does that sound like a guarantee to you?
- A few CCRC contracts offer a guarantee of care for the rest of your life. In these cases, the contract states that if you outlive your resources in independent living, assisted living, or skilled nursing care, they make up the cost difference. These are the best CCRC contracts.

My mom was lucky. Her CCRC had a Good Samaritan Fund. I worked there and knew about the fund, but it was set up so that at any given time only 10 residents could receive help. We were lucky that my mom was one of the 10 who received help. Other residents were not as fortunate as my mom. What will happen to you if you are "number 11" at your community?

Is the rental or buy-in community run as a for-profit or nonprofit?

All senior communities need to run in the black to survive. Nonprofits may seem better, but they are often guided by a board of directors whose members may or may not fully understand the health care needs of seniors.

For example, I worked at a nonprofit CCRC that had a local television personality, a local popular car dealer, and a pastor on its board, none of whom had any health care experience. They tend to be very mission-driven and many believe that nonprofits provide the best care from quality staff. Sadly, even this nonprofit Christian-based CCRC had problems with elder abuse. (I warned you in my introduction that dirty secrets would be exposed!)

For-profits can fall into two categories. Either they are on the stock exchange and are driven by the bottom line for stockholders, or it could be owned by a local or regional business owner who knows the residents by name and treats them as family.

Tip: Ultimately, you want to select a well-run community with a stable ownership and low staff turnover.

Key questions: Here are some great undercover questions to help you learn about the operations of any retirement community.

- Ask who owns the community and how often they visit.
- Are the owners planning on selling the community in the future?
- What is the debt on the community? (The average is $50 to $100 million dollars of debt but debt-free is the best answer.)
- How much does the community pay per month for its mortgage?
- How much have the residents' monthly payments increased each year? Look at a five-year history.
- Are there "extra costs" and what are they?

- How many full-time employees work there? Ask how many part-time employees work there? Relate these numbers to the number of apartments in the community and compare them to each other.
- What is the turnover rate for frontline staff?
- Ask specifically about the longevity of management staff. (The more years on the job, the more stability for the residents.)
- Ask how long the administrator has been working there and how long he or she has been licensed. If the administrator has been working at the community for less than a year, ask about the length of tenure at his or her previous position.

Quality differences between rentals and buy-ins
Quality can be broken into two categories:

1. What you can see when you walk through the building.
2. That which you cannot necessarily see.

Some rental retirement communities are gorgeous. They have the look and feel of a fine hotel with lush landscaped grounds and interior. This is what you can see.

This is what you *can't* see:

- The level of debt and how it will affect your monthly fee increases over the long run;
- The staff turnover rate;
- Whether anyone will be around to help you after a fall;

- If they will help you transition and move to another facility when they can no longer take care of you.

Tip: Many rental communities imply that they will take care of you for life, but read the contract. If they don't provide assisted living and skilled nursing care, they simply don't offer the levels of care that you will need in the future.

Some Continuing Care Retirement Communities (CCRCs) are stunning. They are literally resorts with all the levels of care provided on the same campus. Many have been built recently and accommodate impressive amenities that cater to the younger senior.

This is what you *can't* see:

- Their debt and how it will affect your monthly fee increases over the long run.
- How long most of the staff has worked there. Hint: If it's a brand new building, all the staff are new. I have lived through the operational headache of opening a new CCRC. Prepare yourself for unexpected bumps and changes.
- After you leave the building, whether vertically or horizontally, when will your family be reimbursed the returnable part of the entrance fee (according to the contract)?

Dirty secret exposed: Most CCRCs reimburse the estate only after the apartment has been reoccupied. If there is a downturn in the economy and occupancy wanes, this could take years.

Some CCRCs and retirement communities may look a little dated, but if they have no debt this could mean lower monthly fee increases. Do your homework and don't base your decision on looks alone.

Tip: Nursing quality is not as simple as having a registered nurse (RN) or licensed practical/vocational nurse (LPN/LVN) on site. The community's licensing can restrict what they can do, preventing some nurses in independent living settings from providing even blood pressure checks or basic wound care. Can you believe that? It's true! Make no assumptions.

Key question: A key consideration of quality in the services provided is your family's responsibility in a crisis. What if you need an urgent surgery in the hospital? Ask each retirement community how they would respond in this situation. CCRCs can coordinate with discharge planners and doctors to bring you back to the most independent setting possible. It may mean a few weeks in their skilled nursing care with physical therapy or 30 days of respite care in their assisted living setting until you can return to your independent home. The beauty lies in the choices of care on the CCRC campus where you can be transferred between care levels by the community instead of your family. Many rental communities just wait to find out if you will return so they can continue charging you rent. If you can't return, some will hope that your family will take a while to move out your belongings, so they can continue to charge your family for the rent.

How many levels of care does the rental community or Continuing Care Retirement Community (CCRC) really offer?

Rental communities do not offer all the levels of care and neither do some CCRCs. Some imply that they can take care of you for life, but when you need more care than their licensing typically allows you will either be shipped out to the closest nursing home or be charged extra for caregivers, home health staff, or independent nurses to help you. A CCRC should provide at least three levels of care: independent living, assisted living, and skilled nursing care.

> **Beware:** Some CCRCs and rental communities *say* that they provide nursing care, but really they hire nurses to come to your apartment and charge you an hourly rate. These excessive costs can deplete your assets quickly. Ask questions and go to see all the levels of care they provide before you decide to move in.

It really gets down to what are reasonable and affordable costs over the long run.

Tip: Let me give you an example of what can happen in two retirement communities: Retirement Community A and Retirement Community B. Community A has Lying Luella and Community B has Honest Hannah working for them. Lying Luella did not share all future costs with a potential resident.

Honest Hannah walked each applicant through all the costs of future care. I hope you have an Honest Hannah as your retirement counselor.

Conclusion: Let's look ahead five to 10 years from now

Seniors are living to the ripe old ages of 90 to 110 years of age. Most people sell a home to move to a retirement community. Study these chapters and do lots of homework to determine if a rental community with a month-to-month contract or a Continuing Care Retirement Community (CCRC) is a better option for you.

No one has a crystal ball to determine how many years they are going to live or how long they will need of a higher level of care. My mom ran out of money about half way through a seven-year stay in assisted living. Since she was part of a CCRC with a Good Samaritan Fund, she was not kicked out. A rental community would have required my mom to leave.

The quality and transitioning of future care is an important determining factor in your choice of a senior living community. CCRCs provide multiple levels of care on the same campus and this can make it much easier for your family during a health care crisis. CCRCs usually offer a variety of choices to transition a resident as he or she ages and requires more help, support and care.

Chapter 7
Nine Quick Tips on Selecting the Right Senior Living Retirement Community

1. Trust your first impressions of the community

There are two ways to gain first impressions of retirement communities.

- Slowly and methodically researching multiple communities over a number of years.
- Quickly (within a few days) exploring all the retirement communities in your area.

Tip: When I, with my team members and consultants, mystery shop communities, we find it most effective to tour multiple communities on the same day for several days in a row. Like cream, the best community easily rises to the top.

As you tour communities, you will start seeing differentiating elements emerge:

- The quality of service you witnessed (for example, how the receptionist greets you);
- Do the residents have a lifestyle you want?;
- How happy the staff appears to be;
- The presentation and taste of the food;
- Comparing the size and finishes of apartments (granite countertops, lighting, crown molding, flooring, bathroom fixtures, etc.);
- If and how you were introduced to residents and staff;
- Whether the tour was informative and tailored to your needs or conducted by a pushy, harried, or bored salesperson.

2. Interview several staff members

Meet as many management *and* staff members as possible in all the levels of care. Ask them privately if they enjoy working there and how long they have worked for the organization. Watch their body language and facial expressions when they answer. Listen to what they say and note your impressions as you tour.

In addition:

- If you have any dietary needs, meet the chef and/or dining director.
- Current care concerns? Then meet with the health care administrator.

- Always meet the administrator or executive director to find out how they handle resident concerns and ask for examples.
- Meet the maintenance director and find out how quickly they respond to maintenance requests and if they cost extra. Items such as fixing the plumbing, electrical systems, and air conditioning should be included; hanging pictures, hooking up your computer, and programming your TV may cost extra or require an outside expert.
- Is the activity director a fun person who creates great programming, parties, and outings for the residents? Ask how often such activities occur and if the activity director attends the programs and goes on the outings. If not, ask who does and also meet that staff person.
- Make sure you have at least one exchange with a front line employee such as a dining room server or a housekeeper.
- Observe if you hear them calling residents by name. "Honey" does not count and can come across as disrespectful.

3. **Obtain resident and family testimonials**

Yes, many testimonials are found on the retirement community's website or social media. But I am talking about a live testimonial. Speak with several residents and find out how long they lived there and what they like best and least. If you hang out in the lobby for any amount of time, you can usually meet a visiting family member. Tell them you are considering the community and find out their impressions as a family member. Carefully watch their facial expressions, body language and listen to their tone of voice. Family members typically tell you the real story.

4. Determine the quality of community spaces and amenities

When you explore multiple communities in several days, you notice the variances in quantity and quality of community spaces and amenities. Minimally, they have a dining room and an activity room. As seniors age, it is better to have fewer community spaces.

The dining room in my mom's skilled nursing care community doubles as the activity room. This is good for her because with vascular dementia it took her months to recognize the room. More activity spaces would have been confusing for her. Generally speaking, the higher the level of care provided the fewer community spaces are needed.

Most independent retirement communities have a large space for the entire community to gather for seminars, entertainment, or holiday parties. In smaller communities, the lobby or dining room may be used for these activities.

Communities can have separate rooms for dining, fitness, library, religious services, billiards, cards, and games. They may even have an art studio, theater, lounge, and beauty shop. These spaces will be a part of your future home, so they should feel comfortable to you. Hopefully, there is also a private space where you can meet with your visiting family or friends.

Determine what lifestyle you want and how much variety you enjoy.

Key questions: How big are the community spaces? Are they tastefully decorated and in good repair? If the wallpaper is tattered, ask when they plan on replacing it.

5. Scrutinize the activity program

Ask for an activity calendar and a list of the community's trips for the last several months. Take this home and study it. Is it a lifestyle that you want? Are you witnessing vibrant activities in a variety of community spaces?

Activities can be grouped under a few headings. Here are some questions to consider as you review the activity calendar and community trip list.

Wellness Focus

- Do they have a pool? Is it saline or chorine?
- What is the variety of exercise classes and where do they take place?
- Are the residents charged extra for activity instructors?
- Do they provide good quality exercise equipment that you would use?
- Are monthly wellness seminars scheduled?

Entertainment Events and Parties

- How often do they have live entertainment and is it good quality?
- Is there a social hour at least one day a week?
- Do they have dancing or line dancing?
- Do they have monthly birthday celebrations, a yearly luau or similar large-scale event, Veterans events and anniversary celebrations?

Life-long Learning and Continuing Education

- What are the opportunities for learning and education on and off campus?
- Do staff members or residents get speakers for seminars and educational programs?
- Will you be intellectually stimulated by these programs?

Outings and Trips

- What were the last five trips?
- How many residents participated?
- Would you want to go on these trips?
- Was there an extra cost?
- Ask to go on an outing and see if the seats on the bus are comfortable and the residents are friendly.

6. Examine the social and spiritual connectivity of the residents

- How are new residents welcomed and incorporated into the community?
- What are the seating arrangements for dining venues? (Some places require you to sit in the same chair at the same table each night. This is okay for residents with dementia where routine is beneficial and needed but restricts social connectivity for others.)
- Are the residents cliquey—not open to interacting with newcomers?

- Are the religious services or Bible studies fitting with your beliefs?
- Is transportation available to the worship center or church of your choice?
- Is your faith represented, or will you be ostracized because of your faith choice?

7. Determine if your needs fit within the disclosure of care

(Disclosure of care is a document that specifies what care can be provided at the community.)

- Independent living retirement communities are designed for healthy, active seniors. The resident cannot be a risk to himself, herself or to another resident.
- Assisted living is for people who are independent but need help with the activities of daily living. This support is not designed for a combative resident.
- Secured memory care is for residents with severe dementia or progressed Alzheimer's.
- Skilled nursing facilities offer around-the-clock nursing supervision to take complete care of residents on a short- or long-term basis.

There can be many variations, but these are the four basic levels of care. If *any* care is involved, the community must provide you with a disclosure statement of care so you can see what they will and will not provide as you age.

It is sad when a senior wants to live in an independent setting and is no longer capable of it. For a senior who can barely walk, a smaller community may be easier to navigate.

8. Plan on needing future care

If you move into an independent living setting, you must remember that you will need more support or assistance in the future. Some senior living communities allow you to bring in home care so you don't have to move to an assisted living setting right away and others do not. Some communities have their own trained and qualified caregivers who have had a criminal background check (trained in-house caregiver support is a nice future choice, by the way.)

If you move directly into assisted living, ask if you can bring in additional caregivers at a later period. There is a stage between assisted living and skilled nursing care when additional caregivers would allow you to keep your apartment a little longer, so you won't have to move to skilled nursing care prematurely and potentially share a room.

Ask what transpires in an emergency situation. What happens if you are recovering from a surgery in the hospital and want to come back to your home there? What are your options? Do they offer rehab onsite? Is there an assisted living with a 30-day respite program? Is there a licensed skilled nursing community onsite? Can you use your own caregivers? Does the community offer caregivers in-house? Are the caregivers from an outside agency? What is the cost and the minimum hours?

 Tip and beware: Some retirement communities bring in an outside caregiver company, so when you need a little help, you may have to pay for a four-hour minimum care period.

The range of services for home care, chore services and the availability of a nurse are most important when you need them and this may not seem obvious at the time you are making your choice. It is often a weak area of knowledge for the marketing people. I would be remiss if I did not warn you that some marketing staff members lie on this point. Others are purposely vague or imply future services and support that are not available. All of this is said to convince you to move in. The most common lie that I hear is that you will never have to move again.

Be careful! Ask lots of questions! Make no assumptions!

9. Finances—costs today and in the future

Plan ahead financially. What may sound like the most affordable option today can cost the most in a few months or in a few years when you need more care. My mom initially thought a rental community would be her best financial option. Instead, our family talked her into paying a one-time investment to move into a Continuing Care Retirement Community (CCRC). This was the smartest move ever; she has received a higher level of care for eight years now and ran out of her resources five years ago. She was never kicked out of her CCRC for lack of finances.

Key question: Remember to ask if the CCRC offers a guarantee of care for life. Ask to review the contract. These three words should not follow the guarantee: "At Our Option." "At our option" may not mean "a guarantee."

Conclusion

Be smart and do your homework. It's most effective to tour several communities on the same day. Seniors who plan ahead will have time to research their options, those in crisis mode will find themselves with fewer options.

- Trust your first impressions of the community.
- Interview several staff members.
- Obtain resident and family testimonials.
- Determine quality of community spaces and amenities.
- Scrutinize the activity program.
- Examine the social and spiritual connectivity of the residents.
- Determine if your needs fit within the disclosure of care.
- Plan on needing future care.
- Review your finances looking at costs today and in the future.

Chapter 8
What is the Community Lifestyle *Really* Like?

Sit in the community's lobby for one hour and observe the comings and goings. What do you see? What do you smell? What do you hear? How do the residents interact with each other, the staff, and visitors? Can you picture yourself living there?

Are all the people old and frail at retirement communities? No!

There will be some old and frail people in any community you evaluate. It is a part of life. You may be old and frail and fit right in. Other seniors 90-plus years old are dancing every Saturday night. Some 70-year-old seniors can look gaunt and fragile, but maybe they are recovering from a knee or hip surgery two weeks ago.

What if you are a younger vibrant senior who enjoys exercise, traveling, outings, lifelong learning, card games, and dining with like-minded vibrant people? You may need to do more research to complete your homework.

How to find the vibrant residents

Active residents are harder to spot while touring a retirement community. Why? Because an active senior lives life to the fullest and is probably not at home when you are visiting. You must select the right time for a fair representation of the majority of residents.

Best times to spot vibrant residents

- Early morning in exercise classes or the health club;
- At dinner enjoying social dining;
- At scheduled activities such as line dancing, strength training, tai chi, karaoke, painting, language classes, educational seminars, wood working, card games, and so on.

Why is it hard to spot a vibrant senior resident?

- Healthy seniors have usually completed their exercise or swim class by 9:00 a.m., so, if you tour the community in the late morning or afternoon, you will miss seeing them in the health club or pool.
- Many healthy seniors cook one or two of their meals each day, so they may be at home preparing a gourmet feast.
- Most of them drive or use the community's transportation to go shopping or run errands.
- They tend to take advantage of the scheduled outings, which typically last half the day or longer, so if you tour during a resident trip day, you will miss them.
- Active seniors fill their days with activities, then play cards or watch a movie in the theater after dinner.

- They often take trips on their own and may be on an extended vacation, RV trip, or on a cruise.

Ask for an activity calendar

Retirement communities fall into two groups:

1) They have an exciting calendar with activities and outings that you would enjoy participating in.
2) They are boring and lackluster with few activities.

To determine which type you're visiting, simply read the calendar for every day of the month, studying the outings and exercise classes offered. Think about your own interests. One of my friend's mothers thinks her community is boring because they only offer a few activities per week. But, many of the activities at her community are sports related and she is not interested in sports.

 **Tip: Find out about the quantity and quality of weekend activities when the activity director is not working.**

If you have questions, talk to the activity director. Does he or she seem like a fun person to host events and outings? Is he or she open to new ideas and starting new clubs if there is enough interest?

If you are a bridge player, find out what types of bridge they offer. Is it duplicate or social bridge? Ask to play a couple of times to find out if the residents are friendly and if their card skills match yours.

Check out the bulletin boards for upcoming activities. Are they current or does it hold announcements for an activity that took place two months ago? It better be current.

Tip: Find out if everyone goes to bed after dinner or if scheduled activities are still in full swing in the evenings. Determine which of these alternatives you prefer.

Go on an outing with the residents

Yes, go to the museum or casino, on a cultural excursion to a performing arts center, sports venue, or on whatever trip interests you the most. See how the residents relate to each other and to you on the outing. Are you welcomed or ostracized?

Tip: Ask about costs for outings. Residents typcially pay for the entrance fee into the museum or the ticket for a performance and whatever the cost is for going out to lunch. What varies widely is how much the community may charge for the bus transportation. Most places provide free transport to local venues and only charge for destinations that are one hour or more away.

Ask what other services the retirement community provides

Don't be afraid to ask detailed questions about the services at each retirement community that you explore. You are not always comparing apples to apples here. Don't make an assumption that they all offer the same services.

Tip: Many places decrease the frequency of services to make their monthly fee sound less expensive than competitors. Your costs for electricity, cable TV, housekeeping, and so on may increase your monthly average costs to more than you had thought it would be and another community might have provided better value.

Housekeeping, linens, and maintenance

Housekeeping, linens, and maintenance are fabulous services that we all want. As we age, it gets harder to maintain the same level of cleanliness because of loss of vision, and mobility. Let the staff do all the things that hurt your back, so you can spend your time enjoying yourself. You have worked hard your whole life and you deserve to be pampered. My mom loved these services and the maintenance men became her friends.

Housekeeping frequency

Most retirement communities offer housekeeping, either once a week or once a month. What a fabulous service to enjoy in your retirement. But find out exactly what is included. Usually, a certain amount of time is allotted to each apartment. Find out what that is. Some places don't dust, because they don't want to be liable for any breakage of knickknacks. Most of them mop and vacuum and clean the bathrooms and kitchen. Any detail work on the stove could be extra as is cleaning the inside of the refrigerator. Windows are typically washed twice a year. Ask a lot of questions to find out exactly what each retirement community offers. Remember, some communities charge extra for cleaning services. My mom's Continuing Care Retirement Community (CCRC) only offered monthly cleaning in independent living. Looking back, I wish it had been weekly.

Linen service

Some retirement communities do your linens, either once a week or once per month. This usually includes taking the sheets off your bed, washing them, and remaking your bed. Some places use their own white or off-white sheets. If colored sheets are important to you, you may need to wash your own, but they will change them for you if you ask. Linen service usually includes towels, but ask. My mom's CCRC did not offer linen service until she moved to assisted living. She laundered her own sheets, towels, and clothes in the community laundry room.

Put linen services and personal laundry on your checklist of questions to ask.

Maintenance of apartment homes and campus

Maintenance varies between communities. In general, maintenance staff would be responsible for the community spaces, touch-up painting in the halls, plumbing, electrical, cable TV, apartment renovations, the health club equipment, the swimming pool, and spa. Some places hire landscaping services separately and others roll it into the maintenance department's responsibility.

I have seen retirement communities with 200 apartments and just one maintenance man and others with 250 apartments and six maintenance men, including an air conditioning specialist. Ask about the average response time for a resident maintenance request. How long does it take for maintenance to unplug a toilet or repair the cable box?

 **Tip: Look around when you visit and you can easily see if a community is well maintained. In my experience, well-maintained communities are also usually well run.**

Wi-Fi and Cable TV

These are great benefits. Many communities offer Wi-Fi in the lobby and community spaces. Decide if this works for you as a free Internet service in combination with your laptop. Free Wi-Fi is great for residents who e-mail family and surf the web. If you do online banking and bill paying, public Wi-Fi is not usually recommended and you might want to get your own Internet service.

Having the Internet brought directly to your apartment with a secure connection usually entails an extra expense. It's easy to set up an Internet service with a modem and wireless router.

The cable TV service included in the monthly fee is usually just basic cable, typically offering 40 to 90 stations. A premium movie station or special sports station will usually cost extra.

Many communities will not allow you to have your own TV dish or special cable service. They may contract with a certain company and only that brand is allowed in the building. Perhaps other communities don't want an unsightly cable dish on the balcony. Think about how much and what TV shows you like to watch before you make a decision.

Transportation

Most active seniors don't rate the need for transportation very highly. My mom drove everywhere. Toward the end of her driving days, other retirement community employees reported seeing my mom looking through the steering wheel to drive. She had shrunk and could not see over the wheel. Then she had a fall and could no longer drive. Six months later she gave her car to her granddaughter.

Tip: Changes in driving abilities can happen quickly. You may be laid up when recovering from hip surgery or your vision may take a turn for the worse. Ask how many buses, cars, and drivers the community offers to meet your transportation needs.

Typically, a community with 200 or more apartments will have a bus and two cars. The bus takes groups of residents shopping and on outings. Some places charge a flat fee for gas on outings, depending on the distance traveled. This makes sense when going an hour or more away. My mom loved the outings with other residents. When she was active, she went on every trip that was offered. After her fall, the steps on the bus were too steep for her and she had to curtail one of her favorite pastimes.

Community cars are usually used to drive residents to scheduled medical and dental appointments within a certain radius.

Key questions: Ask what the driving radius is for medical and dental appointments. Are your doctors within the zone or will you need to change doctors? Find out if you can pay extra if your doctor is out of the area. If you want to keep your hairdresser that you have loved for years, how will you get there?

Tip: Transportation pick up and drop off times vary widely. Some retirement communities drop you off at the doctor on time and others will get you there two hours early to accommodate other residents. Sometimes the drivers provide you with a number to call when you are done and pick you

up right away, and at other times you may have to wait for an hour or two. This all depends on the community's budget and how many cars, buses and drivers that the retirement community owns or contracts with.

Security and 24-hour staff

In this day and age retirement communities should have security staff. Ask if all the outside doors are locked all the time except for the front door. Is there a full-time attendant at the front desk, including weekends? What is their policy on visitors coming in to and walking through the building? Usually, guests need to sign in at the desk before visiting with residents.

Some seniors worry about staff going into their apartment when they are not at home. There is a simple solution for this: check the policy at each retirement community. Many will only allow staff to go into a resident apartment in response to an emergency situation, and then they must go in pairs, for security.

All other housekeeping and routine maintenance tasks (such as changing the batteries in the smoke detectors) are scheduled, so you can be home to supervise if you choose.

Retirement communities also provide the benefit of knowing that a responsible person has your key when you are traveling. So you can travel worry free while that responsible person takes care of your place and holds your mail. All you have to do is have fun on your vacation!

What is the Community Lifestyle Really Like?

It is comforting for single seniors to have 24-7 staff. If you can't sleep in the middle of the night, you will always have someone to talk with.

Daily check-in and emergency response

Many retirement communities offer a daily check-in system. This is wonderful. You never have to worry about not being discovered if you have a mishap. If you don't check in, someone will come to your aid and get you any help you may need.

Find out if the community provides an emergency call system or if it costs extra. Many communities have emergency pull cords in the resident's bedroom and bathroom. Others provide emergency call pendents that can be worn. Ask if medically trained staff respond to the emergency call or if they only call 911 to handle a health crisis. It is always best to have medically trained staff available around the clock.

Are pets allowed?

If you have pets, ask if they would be welcomed or not. More and more places are allowing pets though most retirement communities limit the size or quantity of furry pets. If your canine companion is your best friend, know that you may be required to go through a pet interview to determine if the dog is friendly with strangers and would be a good fit for the community. You need to have a strategy or options for how to exercise your furry friend if you become incapacitated. Create a plan for your pal in case you have a medical crisis and are unable to care for your pet.

Conclusion

Are you a vibrant senior that wants to live with other mentally stimulating seniors? Then look around until your gut tells you that you have found your future home. You may just want interesting neighbors in a secure environment with some services. If you decide to move into a community that is only independent living, then remember that you will have to move again when you need more help or care options.

Is it a fun and energetic community? This is easy to see and even better to experience firsthand. Ask for an activity calendar and see if the programming and scheduled trips are to your tastes. Then check for yourself how many residents participate.

Determine what you want your lifestyle to include. Some places cost less and offer fewer services. You get what you pay for. Think about your lifestyle today and what you may need in the coming years.

Chapter 9
Is the Independent Living Community Really Assisted Living in Disguise?

You: "Do you offer independent living?"
Salesperson: "Yes!"

Beware! The salesperson may be lying through his or her teeth. This may or may not be the truth. Keep reading.

You may be "assured" that your new home is independent living. Then you head to the dining room, looking forward to a vibrant dinner conversation. Suddenly you discover that your dining companions are impaired in some significant way.

Do enough research. Many rental communities mingle independent and assisted living residents for dining, activities, entertainment, and outings. The residents may be memory impaired and not able to manage on their own. You could move into a supposed independent community and learn later that it really is assisted living.

Here are your housing choices that might or might not be segregated by a designated area, floor, or building:

- Stand-alone independent living with or without home care;
- Independent living and assisted living combined;
- Independent living, assisted living, and memory care combined;
- Stand-alone assisted living;
- Stand-alone memory care;
- Stand-alone skilled nursing;
- Continuing Care Retirement Communities can have two, three or four levels of care.

Key questions: Ask how many residents get support in their apartment and who provides the care: on-site staff or an outside home care agency? If caregivers are onsite staff, then the community oversees their work. To learn how to work with an outside agency see chapter 3, "The Facts on Home Care."

Home care in an independent retirement community

Individual state licensing can restrict an independent living retirement community's home care services. Many states require a retirement community to create a secondary business to provide home care for residents or to contract with an outside care company to bring personal care to individual residents.

Tip: As you age, you will want to have future care options. What if your care needs fall somewhere between independent living and assisted living? You don't want to have to move prematurely to an assisted living community to get the extra help you need.

Double Tip: A contract between a retirement community and a home care agency is not an endorsement of that company. See chapter 3, "The Facts on Home Care" for suggestions on how to evaluate home care agencies. You get what you pay for! Make sure the caregivers are trained to work with elders and that a criminal background check is performed for all staff. True story: I went through the vetting process to hire a home care company for an independent

retirement community where I worked. But, the administrator decided to select a company based on the minimum hours required for the resident, not the best care.

Independent living licensing

Independent living licensing has evolved over the years to the point that no routine personal care can be provided by staff. The licensing limits what the nurse (if there is one on staff) can provide, though they are allowed to help and respond in emergency situations.

Tip: Some communities have policies that do not allow CPR to be performed, even by a nurse. Ask about the nurse or caregiver's ability to resuscitate residents. Determine if their policy fits with your personal beliefs.

Key questions: Ask if there is a nurse on staff and what they are allowed to do for the residents. Find out what happens when you need a little help or support in your independent apartment home. Do you have to move or does support come to you? How much does it cost? Is it contracted with an outside agency?

Tip: Ask about the retirement community's licensing. Licensing determines what care they can and cannot provide.

Assisted living licensing

Assisted living licensing allows a nurse and caregivers to provide routine care for a resident. A nurse is allowed to do regular blood pressure checks and basic wound care. Services such as medication management, stand-by shower assists, dressing, and cueing (prompting) for meals are usually provided to help residents with one or more of the activities of daily living. A disclosure statement of services is always available for your review.

Key questions: Ask if there is a registered nurse on staff and how many hours they work per day. Find out how many staff are certified caregivers or licensed practical/vocational nurses (LPN/LVN). Find out what happens when you need a little help or support in your assisted living apartment. Does support come to you? What types of care cost extra?

Tip: Some retirement communities license every apartment for assisted living services and others only license some apartments. Determine which licensing will work best for you as you age in place. If you are independent, be aware that your neighbor could be receiving assisted living services. Are independent residents mixed with assisted living residents?

Memory care licensing

Memory care is typically licensed as either assisted living or skilled nursing care.

Skilled nursing care licensing

Skilled nursing licensing is extensive. Nurses are on site around the clock. They support post-surgery residents as well as long-term care patients. Many such facilities provide on-site rehabilitation including physical, occupational, and speech therapy. But the services vary. For example, some allow feeding tubes to be administered and others do not. Some end-of-life measures also vary from community to community.

Hospice in independent living

Higher levels of care, such as assisted living and skilled nursing care, almost always allow hospice, when seniors are near the end of life. Find out if the retirement community you are considering allows hospice in their setting. You may or may not want this available.

Conclusion

Maybe you are not as vibrant as you once were. If so, you may benefit from a smaller apartment with more assistance and services to accommodate your needs.

Before making your decision, determine if the senior living community is appropriate for both your current and future living situations.

Ultimately, some retirement communities claim to be independent living and are really assisted living communities in disguise. If you are healthy and active, do your research to find a place with seniors similar to you. It's all about the lifestyle.

Chapter 10
Before You Decide: Try the Food and Tour Many Times

When you visit, look around. Try the food and make sure there are multiple dining options. Anyone could get bored with eating at the same restaurant for the rest of his or her life. I hope the community you are looking at has a variety of dining choices and great menus.

Eat in every dining venue they offer several times and ask these questions:

- Does the food taste good?
- Is the presentation beautiful? (One of my favorite chefs says, "The first taste is always with the eyes.")
- Are there fresh flowers and linens on the table?
- How comfortable are the chairs and the height of the table? (Some chairs are too heavy for seniors to pull out from the table.)
- Can you stab a piece of lettuce with the fork and cut a steak with the knife? (One retirement community reported having a resident revolt about the new silverware. It was not eating friendly—funny, but true.)

- Is the chef willing and able to accommodate your dietary requirements?
- How much variety is there on the menu? (There should be a minimum of three or four selections—14 entrees is the greatest variety I have encountered.)
- How often does the menu change or repeat itself? (Good places create variety by only repeating the menu every five or six weeks.)
- Is the fish fresh?
- Do they use organic fruits and vegetables?
- What is their policy on salt in the food and soup?
- Are the baked goods made on site?
- How much of the menu is prepared from scratch, like home cooking? (95 percent or better is always great!)

Holiday Dining (and I don't just mean Christmas)

- Do they have special holiday menu items?
- Will there be special touches, such as an ice sculpture?
- Are your family members welcome to join you? What will this holiday meal cost?
- Is it a buffet?
- Do they have a turkey, ham, or roast beef carving station?

Theme Dining

The best places have at least one themed dinner a month, such as:

- Chinese New Year.
- Italian night.

- Scandinavian night.
- St. Patrick's Day Irish food.
- Mother's Day Brunch.
- Cinco de Mayo.
- Father's Day Brunch.
- Fourth of July Barbeque.
- French cuisine for Bastille Day.
- German food for Oktoberfest.
- Thanksgiving feast with all the trimmings.
- Hanukkah and other Jewish celebrations.
- Christmas dinner.
- New Year's Eve formal dinner.
- Super Bowl tailgate party food.

Alcohol

- Can you order alcohol in the dining room? How much does it cost?
- Are you allowed to bring your own wine bottle?
- Is there a corkage fee?
- Will they provide glasses?
- Is it ever complimentary?
- Maybe you prefer an alcohol-free community?

Dine with residents

Ask residents about the quantity and quality of the food.

- Are they happy with the food and the chef?
- Do cliques of residents always dine together or do they welcome new residents?

- What types of dining companions have they enjoyed?
- Does the dining staff know the residents' names?
- Is the seating assigned or can they can dine with whomever they wish?
- Is the dining room vibrant with conversation?

 **Tip: Observe what the other residents are wearing. Is the dining attire too formal or too casual for your tastes? Some seniors love dressing up for dinner each evening. Do you? Are ties required? Or do you prefer a more casual dining atmosphere?**

Drop in unannounced and look around the dining room

- Are lunch and dinner treated equally? Or, is the big meal at noon with sandwiches for dinner?
- How many people are dining alone?
- Do residents talk to one another and enjoy social connectivity?
- Is there energy in the room?
- Are the residents happy, sad, or nonexpressive?

Before You Decide: Try the Food and Tour Many Times

Additional questions to ask

- How flexible are the dining hours?
- Is there a dress code in the dining room? Can someone come to breakfast with curlers in their hair or wear sweats at dinner?
- If it is a Continuing Care Retirement Community (CCRC), does the independent dining room kitchen prepare food for assisted living and skilled nursing? If the kitchen is separate at the assisted living or skilled nursing, you may want to sample that food too.
- How long has the chef worked at the community?
- Is the dining staff comprised of high school or college students? How do you feel about that? Most seniors love associating with young people at dinner. Is there a scholarship fund developed for their future education? (If so, the dining staff can continue working through college.)
- Do they celebrate resident birthdays? How?
- Can you have guests to dine? What is the cost?
- How much do additional meals cost for a resident?
- If you miss a meal, can you make it up later in the month?
- Can you buy a banana, quart of milk or an egg on a regular basis as at a convenience store?
- Do they offer room service and if so how much does it cost?
- What happens if you are sick and can't go to the dining room?

Tip: Some senior living communities offer dining throughout the day, which can be good or bad. If you enjoy eating at nontraditional times, it can be good. But when residents eat at random times, they often end up dining alone, losing out on the social connection provided when everyone dines together. The other challenge is how the kitchen operates. If the special for the day is spaghetti and you want to eat at 3:00 p.m., will the lunch pasta be soggy or stuck together? How do they maintain freshness and quality throughout the day?

Conclusion: How to determine if the community provides good or great dining

Any retirement community can have great, good, fair, or horrible food. Remember to try every dining venue several times and determine the quality for yourself. The timing of the big meal of the day could be a deal breaker for you. For me, it is about the entire dining experience: the table linens, the presentation and taste of the food, menu variety, fresh ingredients, and extra details—such as a lemon slice in the water glass, offering wine or alcohol, the quality of service, attention to a special dietary request, and engaging servers who check back to see if everything is to your satisfaction. Oh, and a great baker who offers a variety of luscious desserts is important too.

Chapter 11
"It's too Expensive to Move!"

At one time the Masons had an asset surrender program in exchange for lifetime care. Many seniors heard about this and still assume they have to turn over all their assets to receive life care. This asset surrender program ended in 1995 according to the Ohio Masonic Home.[15]

Is it really too expensive to move?

When most seniors add up their yearly expenditures and divide by 12 to get a monthly average, they learn it can be less expensive to live year-round in a retirement community that provides daily nutritious meals. A spreadsheet with your total expenditures over a five- to ten-year period can show you the real costs of maintaining your home (don't forget such home improvement projects as a new roof, siding repair, and painting). What are your real costs living at home now? Do you own a home? If so, you have choices. If not, you may have fewer alternatives.

---

15 The Ohio Masonic Home—online frequently asked questions

FACT: 12.9 percent of seniors live in poverty[16]

This amounts to one in eight seniors living below the poverty level, using the 2012 supplemental poverty measure (SPM) that includes health care costs. Thirteen states have higher poverty rates than the national average using the SPM: California, Colorado, Connecticut, Florida, Hawaii, Illinois, Maryland, Massachusetts, Nevada, New Hampshire, New Jersey, New York, and Virginia.[17]

Poverty level choices for independent living

The sad truth is that many seniors cannot afford to move to a retirement community with all the wonderful amenities. They may still qualify for government subsidized housing under the Department of Housing and Urban Development or in a Section 8 Retirement Community.[18] Government subsidized senior living communities only take a portion of a senior's monthly income. Typically, meals are not included. Some have community spaces for neighbors to gather and others do not. There are long wait lists—sometimes two years or longer so you *must* plan ahead.

Will some of our seniors become homeless because they took a reverse mortgage on their home or can't afford to live there any longer? Or because they can't afford to rent an apartment and Section 8 housing is full? This will be a massive problem in the United States in the coming years, especially as the baby boomers age.

---

16   12.9 percent includes the Supplemental Poverty Measure (SPM) released by the U.S. Census Bureau, www.census.gov/prod/2013pubs/p60-247.pdf

17   www.census.gov/prod/2013pubs/p60-247.pdf

18   www.portal.hud.gov/hudportal/HUD?src=/topics/rental_assistance

Poverty level choices for assisted living

Our country must provide alternatives for seniors who have worked hard their whole lives and now need assistance with the activities of daily life, such as bathing, dressing and medication management.

The government provides only low reimbursements for assisted living so it is difficult to find a subsidized assisted living community. Christian organizations that offer assisted living options often provide a Good Samaritan Fund to existing residents who qualified financially upon move-in. But this is not a guarantee of care!

A Medicaid assisted living community is difficult to find, and if you do find one, it may not provide the best quality of care. This is the sad truth. Some of them simply don't have enough money from the government to run a thriving community.

My own mom ran out of her resources in assisted living. She was blessed that she had made a one-time investment in a Continuing Care Retirement Community (CCRC) with a Good Samaritan Fund. So, even though she could not make the whole monthly payment, she was not kicked out. This was a nongovernment fund. But she was lucky—she was tenth on the list of 10 to qualify for this subsidy program. What if she had been number 11?

Poverty level choices for skilled nursing care

Unfortunately, I am all too familiar with this scenario. As I write this, my mom is in this situation. She only has $2,000 to her name and does not have enough income to pay the monthly fee at her community. Her Social Security, pension, and annuity are simply not enough.

Medicaid is currently available at most skilled nursing communities. The government reimbursements are not enough to cover costs, but the good communities can usually make up the difference through private patients. An astonishing number of skilled nursing communities have closed because of the poor reimbursement from the government for destitute seniors.

It costs a significant amount of money to feed, clothe, house and care for a vulnerable senior 24-hours a day, day after day, month after month. My mom has been subsidized through Medi-Cal for 18 months as I write this. She has vascular dementia which has created tremendous anxiety for her and debilitating memory loss. She is vulnerable and needs help with absolutely everything.

Is your home your main asset?

If you have a home, way to go! You worked hard your whole life to earn it. Hopefully, it is paid off and has increased significantly in value. It's wonderful to see seniors with homes that cost $30,000 many decades ago now valued at $500,000 or more. Depending on the value of your home and your monthly income, you may or may not qualify to move to a nice retirement community that provides meals, amenities, an activity program, and emergency call system.

Fifty-five-plus mobile home parks or condominiums

A less expensive alternative for some independent seniors is moving to a 55-plus mobile home park. Seniors can walk or drive a golf cart to attend social activities within the community when they no longer drive.

This type of community does not normally provide daily meals, so a senior's nutrition can be poor. This can lead to dramatic health challenges as they age.

When memory starts to fail, incorrect medication management will be a major factor contributing to an overall health decline in a senior.

These communities do not have a nurse on staff or an emergency call system. Nor do they provide transportation to medical appointments. This type of move is only a Band-Aid, not a cure.

Even a senior who no long drives may be able to have a social life if programs are offered at that community. Condominiums and 55-plus communities vary widely in the number and kind of activities offered, and some offer none at all.

"But, they'll take all my Social Security!"

Fortunately, the days in which a CCRC required a senior to sign over every asset, all monthly income, and the shirt off their back are long gone.

If a one-time investment is required to join the community, some portion may be returnable to you or your estate when you pass away, depending on length of stay at the community.

If you can't pay for your care needs through your assets and monthly income, like my mom, it's a blessing to turn over the Social Security for the care. Think about it, for just your Social Security, you will receive all meals and medications, an emergency call system, utilities, housing, and transportation. This system only leaves my mom $35 a month for such incidentals as getting her hair done and personal laundry.

"Can I still leave my heirs an estate?"

Well, the answer might be yes, if you have enough to take care of yourself for the rest of your life with some left over for your heirs. I have heard stubborn seniors proclaim, "I don't want to pay an entrance fee, because I want my children to get the money." Then, I often see the conclusion of their decision...bringing in expensive home care costing $18,000 a month and watching their assets disappear quickly. At some point, you have to pay for your care—don't be penny-wise and pound-foolish.

Other sources of money to pay for future care

Medicare Part A (Hospital Insurance) helps cover:[19]

- Inpatient care in hospitals;
- Inpatient care in a skilled nursing facility (not long-term care);
- Hospice care;
- Home health care;
- Inpatient care in a religious nonmedical health care institution.

Medicare Part A helps to pay for temporary skilled nursing days with a qualified hospital stay. It can pay for *up* to 100 days of skilled nursing care (as long as you are improving and had a qualifying hospital stay first.)

---

19 www.medicare.gov/Pubs/pdf/10050.pdf

Caution: Sometimes it is hard to determine if a hospital has technically admitted you or not. After two or three days, you may think you qualify for up to 100 days of skilled nursing care to be paid for by Medicare or your private insurance coverage and later you are shocked to be billed for the entire amount. Make sure that you or your power of attorney (POA) has determined that you had a qualifying hospital stay before you get discharged.

Double caution: Medicare does not cover long-term care in a skilled nursing facility.

Medicaid

"Medicaid nursing home coverage pays all of the costs of nursing homes for those who are eligible except that the recipient pays most of his or her income toward the nursing home costs, usually keeping only $66.00 a month for expenses other than the nursing home."[20]

It is difficult to find an assisted living community that accepts Medicaid. Most skilled nursing communities do accept Medicaid. You or your family will need to fill out a mountain of paperwork to qualify for this aid. There is some uncertainty as to how long the government can keep paying for this program.

To find out if you qualify for Medicaid go to www.healthcare.gov.

---

20 www.en.wikipedia.org/wiki/Medicaid

Veterans affairs (VA) benefits

Veterans affairs (VA) benefits, also known as the Aid and Attendance Program, are available to qualifying veterans or surviving spouses. Your assets must be spent down to a certain level and you must need help with several activities of daily living, such as medication management or bathing assistance.

For more information visit www.va.gov.

Long-term care insurance

Congratulations if you planned ahead and included long-term care insurance in your portfolio.

Review your policy. Most cover home care, assisted living, and skilled nursing. If you have had your policy for decades, the benefits may not cover home care, because this benefit did not exist when these policies were first established.

Typically, your long-term care insurance will specify either a maximum dollar amount or time that it will cover. For example, it may state that it will pay for skilled nursing care for three years. If you go beyond three years of care, this benefit will end. Or, if you exceed the stated maximum dollar amount of coverage, it will end. Some seniors have a long-term care insurance policy that has unlimited coverage, but these are rare.

Caution: Recently, I have heard of several seniors whose premium for unlimited long-term care insurance was going to double. Seniors are living longer now and insurance companies can't afford the future liability of offering unlimited coverage.

Dirty Secret Exposed: I know a senior who was denied her long-term care coverage in skilled nursing because she had missed one payment while ill. She and her family are panicked and appealing the decision. Make sure that you have scheduled automatic payments for your premium overseen by someone with your power of attorney.

My mom needed assisted living for seven years. She did not have long-term care insurance, but if she had, it would have run out due to the time limit clause and possibly the dollar amount clause.

Again, check your policy and congratulations for having it! It can really help financially when one spouse is still independent and the other needs substantial care. It protects the healthy spouse as all the assets are not drained for the care of the ill spouse. It can help widows and widowers by preserving a bigger estate for their heirs as well.

Tip: Let your children or whoever has power of attorney know that you have this benefit. I have heard of families that paid for care because they did not know the parent had long-term care insurance. Please inform others of your benefits before you become incapacitated.

"It's too Expensive to Move!"

"My HMO will take care of me."

Your HMO covers doctors, hospitalization and possibly short-term skilled nursing care. It does not cover long-term care needs in assisted living or skilled nursing care.

Conclusion

Nationally, 12.9 percent of seniors are at the poverty level.

Many other seniors claim to be poor when they have a paid-off home and a portfolio of other assets to sustain their future. If this is your situation, then you have choices. Choose wisely. If you wait for a crisis, the assets that you did not want to part with can be depleted quickly when you need higher levels of care.

You will not be able to access many additional sources of money (such as VA benefits or Medicaid) until you have used up your assets.

Chapter 12
In Denial and Waiting for a Crisis

Intellectually, you know that you should move before a health crisis happens. You may have watched your neighbor, a relative, or a friend wait too long. But are you refusing to make a decision about yourself? I have seen this scenario with so many seniors. Hardest of all is when families warn their senior relatives of the risks and dangers of staying in their own home. The seniors may listen and partially agree, yet they still don't act until there is a crisis. Decisions made in crisis mode offer fewer choices and bring unnecessary stress for all parties concerned.

Crisis mode for seniors with adult children

The following are two true stories that I want to share with you. The first is about a couple in their late 80s and the other is about a 90-year-old widow. All three waited until a crisis happened before making a decision about their care.

Example 1: An independent couple with all five of their children nearby

The first story is my own, it's about my in-laws.

They were a vibrant couple in their early 80s. My mother-in-law, Amy, is a colon cancer survivor, gardener, and peace activist. My father-in-law, Bill, is a salt-of-the-earth-type guy, with a gentle spirit, who gave up drinking 15 years ago. They walked everywhere, were both fabulous cooks, and organized a regular Tuesday family luncheon that brought our family together.

Ten years ago, they stopped hosting family gatherings on Christmas and the Fourth of July. Then my mother-in-law began to show signs of memory loss about seven years ago. I saw my own mother's progression of memory loss repeated in my mother-in-law. I would not wish it on anyone. Amy became very frustrated by her memory problems and we would have deep talks about it together. It reassured her to know that she was not the only one going through this.

Bill was the strong one. He covered for Amy by either denying her memory loss or ignoring it.

Losing a child

The pivotal change came when my brother-in-law, Fletch, died of accidental carbon monoxide poisoning. It was horrible and made no sense; the favorite, fun son was gone in a moment.

It's hard to watch a vibrant senior couple deteriorate so quickly.

Losing a child can wipe out anyone's energy and spirit, but from my observation it is especially devastating for seniors. Unfortunately, this happens more often than you might imagine. Amy started sleeping most the time and began isolating herself. All their social connections evaporated almost overnight. Bill was still going to his AA meetings and the family luncheon on Tuesdays, but Amy missed more and more luncheons. Bill continued making excuses for her.

Heart-to-heart discussions

My husband, Chris, and I tried on many occasions to have a heart-to-heart discussion with them about their future needs and options. Amy was getting to the point where she was no longer independent. If something happened to Bill, she would not be able to live on her own.

Chris and I explained that if something happened to my father-in-law, then the family would have to sell the house and move Amy to a senior living community that could provide support and caregivers. Bill claimed he understood this.

Finally, after a fall and an episode of pneumonia, Amy was sent to the hospital. She was completely disoriented and talking gibberish. We were forced to have a meeting with Bill to make him face reality. The conclusion? Bill said, "I understand that I am choosing to wait until there is a crisis. I don't want to move." Well, we did and said everything we could, but we couldn't force this couple, who refused to face reality, to move.

Meanwhile, Chris (the oldest son) and I moved to California for our careers. We were now 1,000 miles away from his parents who were not doing well. This added to the stress for all concerned.

One day Chris called his dad and learned that a man had approached his mom in the yard about selling the family home. It sounded like my in-laws were thinking of putting it on the market in just a couple of weeks. We jumped on a plane to Seattle to make sure they did not get bamboozled on the house deal and to help them find a great retirement community that would be appropriate for them. When we sat down to have a heart-to-heart with them, they innocently said they had no intention of moving. My husband Chris was angry. He said that he came to help and they said they were fine.

My mother-in-law finally said that she would consider moving to a retirement community that provided meals and entertainment. She was tired of just talking to Bill because he never talked back or he could not hear her. (They both have hearing aids.) She knew that her husband would never move.

I could not believe that Amy had asked to move and Bill had refused. If something happened to him, she would not be able to manage on her own. He felt it was his responsibility to take care of her for life. He said, "This is my cross to bear." Bill has macular degeneration and he can barely see to drive. He was making an unsafe choice to stay in the family home and just get by.

Impaired quality of life

They had reached a point where they had a very poor quality of life. Bill was a full-time caregiver for Amy. She never came out of the house except to go to the doctor. Bill would only go to the grocery store when she was sleeping. He was exhausted and deteriorating before our eyes. It broke our hearts. My husband and I are in the senior housing business and they would not listen to us. Talk about the cobbler's children going barefoot!

Continual crisis

Now, one year later, crisis after crisis is happening. Amy's memory loss has progressed to the point that she is verbally hostile to her daughter and her anxiety was so inconsolable that Bill had to call 911. The paramedics were able to calm her down, and after this incident, she was put on medication for her memory loss and anxiety.

Did this incident make Bill face reality? No! Bill continues to say they are fine and he can take care of Amy and drive her to the doctor. In reality, he is scared to drive, because he got lost once and had to ask for directions to get home. How many more such incidences have to occur before they finally face reality?

As I write this, my in-laws are considering getting some help in their home, but Bill does not want to spend the money. Amy asked her daughter if she would be their caregiver. The daughter said, "No, it is too hard for family to toilet other family members." Amy said, "Good, can I have a male caregiver then?" (She still has her sense of humor.)

Their life has become a vicious cycle of Amy's doctor visits to help her dementia and keep her calm, while Bill is afraid to drive because of his macular degeneration and fear of getting lost. Chris flew to Seattle for the funeral of his best friend and spent the rest of his time off with his parents. He found out that his dad really did think he was running out of money: he could not remember how much income he had per month. Between memory loss and macular degeneration, it is very difficult for him to read the tiny print on bank statements, even with a magnifying glass, let alone understand and remember what it all means.

Trouble paying bills

Bill thought he made half per month of what he is really bringing in. Chris went through a year's worth of financial information, checked it twice and proved to his dad that he is spending less per month than what he makes. My father-in-law is relieved. Finally, they will consider hiring caregivers for Amy in order to give his dad a four-hour break twice a week. Bill admitted that he has had no social life for the last two years because of the time he has to spend caring for his wife.

Three of the four remaining children accept their mom's dementia. All four are worried about their dad, but astonishingly won't acknowledge that it is not safe for him to live on his own. My husband discussed taking on the power of attorney for his parents' finances. His dad agreed but then refused to sign the paperwork. His dad thought that he would lose control of his life. My husband only wanted a plan in place for the future. This paperwork can only be signed while Bill is mentally capable of making such decisions.

Tip: Adult siblings rarely agree on elder care for their parents.

Double tip: Power of attorney paperwork should be completed before a health care crisis.

Running out of options

This is an example of a couple who waited too long, leaving the entire family unnecessarily confused, frustrated, stressed, and stuck in crisis mode. What if my in-laws had no kids to rally around them? What would their lives be like then? Even so, they are rapidly running out of choices. Neither is fully independent. They both need assisted living or assisted living with memory care. They are no longer capable of selling their home and moving themselves. Ultimately, they have given up their freedom to choose and now the family will be forced to choose for them and put them some place safe.

Example 2: An independent widow with only one son who lives far away

My good friend Brian's mom, Dorothy, has been a widow for 20 years, is fully independent, and is a very feisty, stubborn senior. She drove every day to the local pool to go swimming, was a fabulous cook, and loved playing cards with her friends.

The first pivotal moment came a few years ago when Dorothy could not pass her driver's license test. She could no longer drive to her social engagements and her isolation began. Friends took her to the grocery store and for necessities, but swimming and card playing became a thing of the past.

The second pivotal moment came when Dorothy fell outside of her home on the Minneapolis ice in zero degree weather. She called out for help and no one answered. Brian's mom was literally lying on the sidewalk with a dislocated shoulder and a very bruised hip. She had her cell phone in her pocket, but at 93 years of age could not figure out how to call 911 on the flip phone. Luckily she had her wireless house phone in her pocket and was able to call 911 for help.

Brian flew from Portland, Oregon to Minneapolis to help his mom. What a burden for an adult child to be responsible for an aging parent who lives far away.

Dorothy's doctor highly recommended a rehab community. Brian checked his mom into the rehab and went back to her house to sleep. Guess what happened? His mom called him at 4:00 a.m., pleading, "Get me out of here!"

"Just go in your diaper."

This is what prompted that phone call. When his mom hit the call light to go to the bathroom, a very pregnant caregiver appeared and claimed, "I can't lift you. Just go in your diaper." Later, when Brian's mom hit the call light again for some ice water, another caregiver appeared and said, "You still have water left in your glass. Drink that first." Then the caregiver just walked away.

In the morning, when Brian's mom complained to the head nurse, the response was angry excuses. Brian's mom then called her doctor who had recommended this rehab center. Fortunately, the doctor took appropriate action. The administrator apologized in person and the head nurse suddenly changed her attitude. Brian's mom was promised that she would never have to be with those two night caregivers again.

It's hard to believe that a 93-year-old, mentally sharp senior had to shake up this Minneapolis rehab community. I wonder how the other residents fared with these "caring caregivers."

Advocating

A month later Dorothy is still in rehab and her only son has been in Minneapolis away from his family for a month. If he were not in Minneapolis advocating on her behalf, she would not have received dignity, timely care, and respect. Dorothy learned that caregivers can retaliate against patients who criticize them. If you are dependent on someone else to feed and toilet you, there may be a fear of voicing a complaint.

Other problems also came up. For example the surgeon never came back to take the staples out of her shoulder so that the rehab could begin in a timely fashion. Brian had to advocate for his mom to make sure the staples would be removed.

Brian reached a point where he had to leave his mom in Minneapolis and fly back home for one week to be with his bride and take care of his taxes. Then he had to fly back to be with his mom for one more month. Thank goodness he had retired just about two months before Dorothy's fall. Would he have been able to take this much time from work to help her? As it is, he has to dip into *his* retirement savings to fund these travel expenses.

I shared with Brian the five possible outcomes for his mom:

1. She could get better and go back home to live independently in her Minneapolis home.
2. She could go home with home care and therapy.
3. She might need to move to an assisted living community that provided support locally in Minneapolis.
4. He could bring her back to Portland to live independently.
5. He could bring her back to Portland to live in an assisted living community and be a local advocate for her.

Heart-to-heart meeting

Brian had a heart-to-heart meeting with his mom. He told her that he did not have the money or time to fly to Minneapolis every time she had a health crisis. His preference was for him to help her sell the family home in Minneapolis and move back to Portland to be near him and his family. Like many seniors, she is a stubborn woman and does not want to give up her home and her friends in Minneapolis. Sadly, her quality of life is diminished because of decreased independence and she is creating a very stressful situation (emotionally and financially) for her only child and his family.

Home care Band-Aid

Brian's mom may have caregivers come to help her transition back into her independent Minneapolis home. Who will be there to manage the caregivers when she is in a weakened state? Her only child is in Portland.

> **Caution:** Not planning ahead left Dorothy in a vulnerable situation dependent on caregivers who can take advantage of her. Plan ahead so this doesn't happen to you.

Crisis mode for seniors with no children

So, what happens if you don't have children? You then have to rely on whoever has your power of attorney or a lawyer who will have to put you some place because you have waited too long. Who will be your advocate at that place?

Conclusion

Do you see yourself in any of these stories? Don't fool yourself. Face reality. We will all eventually be in one of these types of stories if we don't plan ahead.

Be careful...plan ahead and don't wait for a health crisis!

Here are your choices:

1. Choose a supportive environment for yourself as you age.
2. Wait until you have an inevitable health care crisis and have limited choices.

I hear stories like these all the time. You must have an advocate when you are in a vulnerable health crisis.

Chapter 13
What are Your Options if
You Have Waited too Long?

This chapter will cover four crisis scenarios:

Scenario A: for a single senior with dementia.

Scenario B: for a single senior with physical challenges.

Scenario C: for a couple when one is cognitively competent and
the other has dementia or physical challenges.

Scenario D: for a couple who both have dementia.

Scenario A: for a single senior with dementia

When I called my friend Alice, she told me her doctor had just diagnosed her with dementia. I had known about her dementia for two years, because I can easily recognize the early signs from seeing my mom and my mother-in-law suffer through this ugly disease. When someone has worked in the senior care industry for as long as I have, this scenario is all too familiar.

Alice confided that she has started to look at senior housing options and estimates that she can spend two or three more years in her home with its lovely 180-degree view of the Puget Sound. I gently said, "No, Alice, you don't have that much time." She immediately responded, "What? Well, the neighbor down the street said that I could just have someone live in my extra room and take care of me." Again, as kindly as I could, I said, "No, Alice, that is not a good idea."

Now, I had her attention. With a tremor in her voice, Alice asked, "Diane, you are my friend, have been in the senior housing business for years, and I trust you. What do you suggest I do?" Her vulnerability touched me. I treated her with dignity and respect and told her, "Alice, you have been forgetful for several years. Do you remember when you asked me to let you know when it was time to move to a retirement community?" Even though a couple of years had passed since that conversation, she did remember. I continued, "That time is now. Dementia is a progressive disease and you have already had it for several years. Let's walk through your choices. I love you and will help you."

 **Tip: Perhaps my dialogue with Alice will help you to realize that you may be in the same situation. I recommend having a conversation on this topic with someone you love or trust.**

Suggestion: When I refer to Alice, substitute your name and see if the situation fits.

Choice 1: Stay at home and bring in home care help

For several reasons, bringing in home care is not a good idea, especially if you have dementia and are living alone. Let me be as honest with you as I was with Alice.

1. As your dementia progresses, you can become isolated in your home with a single caregiver. There is no social interaction with multiple people who can help you in slowing the progression of your dementia.

2. As your cognition declines, you will become more vulnerable. This caregiver, whom you have trusted and brought into your home, can take advantage of you or your finances. Home care agency management does not provide daily oversight of their staff. You *must* have a nearby adult child or your appointed power of attorney managing the caregiver on a daily, or at least weekly, basis. Alice's children are scattered around the world and are busy with careers and their own families. It would be impossible for them to manage caregivers for her.

3. When you get to the point where you need 24-hour home care, it can become cost-prohibitive for most seniors, including Alice. Most people can't afford $18,000 a month or more to have a 24-hour reputable caregiver from an agency working in their home.

 **Tip: The helpful neighbor down the street, who suggested using short-term home care, is only coming up with a Band-Aid solution when a tourniquet is needed. My friend Alice has about six months to make a decision to set herself up in a safe protective environment for the rest of her life.**

Choice 2: Move to a month-to-month rental facility

Alice has a strong monthly income but limited assets. She is a candidate to choose a rental facility, which does not require a buy-in. There are pluses and minuses with this solution.

Most rental facilities offer independent living, assisted living, or a combination of the two. If your care goes beyond their scope of service, you will be asked to leave, period. This could put Alice in a difficult position several years down the road unable, because of her dementia, to select the next level of care, which could be either memory care or skilled nursing. Alice would be leaving herself open for someone else to choose where to put her.

Tip: Alice does not need to move into a memory care community right now. She just needs to be in a supportive environment with medication management. Hopefully, this community will help her transition to the next level of care. (It is one thing for salespeople to make a promise of future support and quite another to have staff in place two or three years from now who will fulfill the salesperson's promise.)

Double tip: In my experience, the more levels of care a rental facility offers, the less independent are the residents in the independent living portion.

In many areas of the country where I have had experience, I only know of a few rental facilities that could offer Alice a secured memory care area in the future that is a vibrant place for her to live now.

Choice 3: Move to a Continuing Care Retirement Community (CCRC)

Since I have worked in the senior living industry in Seattle for 14 years, I am very familiar with the senior living choices that Alice has. CCRCs that promise to help someone transition to the next level of care are too expensive for Alice. But even though Alice doesn't have a home to sell, she need not despair. There are some affordable CCRCs.

 **Tip: If you have an asset, such as a home to sell, a reputable CCRC is an excellent choice if you are a single senior with forgetfulness or have been diagnosed with early dementia. The bad news is that you may not qualify because of your cognitive decline. This is why it is critical to not wait too long. A health and financial assessment is required to qualify for this type of community.**

Currently, I work at two amazing CCRCs in California that Alice could afford and for which she could qualify. However, she would need to make a move quickly before her cognition declines further and while she can still manage a move.

Tip: A CCRC typically has three or four levels of care on the same campus. They are designed to transition you to the next level of care. Staff is in place to make this happen. This is a part of their mission and what they do for residents on a daily basis.

Scenario B: for a single senior with physical challenges

Your options are slightly different. My friend Brian is currently assessing this situation with his mom, Dorothy, and he too contacted me for trusted advice. This is difficult for everyone, but especially for long distance family members, such as Brian, who lives in Portland, and his mom, who lives in Minneapolis. My heart went out to both of them as I walked Brian through his mom's choices. It wasn't just about where she could reside to recuperate from her fall but also about the long-term financial ramifications.

Red hot tip: It is critical that you consider your short-term and long-term goals simultaneously when making your care decision. Review your finances carefully. If you start dipping into your assets too aggressively to take care of your short-term care needs, you may limit your long-term choices down the road.

Let's walk through your options.

Choice 1: Stay at home and bring in help

This is the choice that Brian's mom wants to make. Dorothy has been in a rehab community for six weeks, recovering from a bad fall on the ice and snow of Minneapolis. All she wants is to go home. This is what most people want. She cannot use one of her arms and she needs a walker. Her son sees the reality of her situation. Will she be able to cook, cut her own food, dress herself, shower, wash her hair, get groceries, empty the trash (which requires managing steps), wash her clothes downstairs in the basement, and socialize with others?

Her Medicare coverage for her rehab stay is about to expire and the discharge planners are trying to fulfill the "resident's wish" to go home. So, they are offering home care solutions. Can this help her in the short-term? Yes, of course. Will it eat up her limited assets? The answer to this is also yes, of course! Will she ever get back to her old vivacious self, fully independent in her own home? Rehab facilities often try to give their patients a glimmer of hope. In my opinion, Dorothy's days of being fully independent are history.

Tip: Home care is a fantastic solution if you need it on a temporary basis and you are cognitively able to manage the caregiver. Home care usually comes with a four-hour per day minimum requirement and you may be able to get by with a caregiver for four hours a day, two to seven days a week. The caregivers could provide you with a stand-by

shower assist, set up meals for you to microwave the rest of the week, buy your groceries, wash your dishes, do your laundry, and empty the trash. They may or may not do light housekeeping. But who is going to clean your bathroom, change your sheets, dust, vacuum, mop your kitchen floor, take you to the hairdresser, cut your toenails, and take care of your yard? If you have a pet, there are even more chores to be done.

Red hot tip: If you need home care on a long-term basis, it can wipe out your limited assets and deny you the opportunity to move into a great community of your choosing that can support your care needs the rest of your life.

Choice 2: Move to a month-to-month rental facility

If you have only physical challenges, as Dorothy does—even if you think they are temporary—and you have a good monthly income, a rental community could be a good option for you. Refer to my earlier chapters on how to find a good community that suits your needs. When you need a higher level of care, which the rental facility does not provide, then you can go out with a friend or family member and shop for those options.

In my friend Brian's case, that would mean yet another trip from Portland to Minneapolis for him. If your son or daughter is still working, they would have to give up at least another week of their vacation time to help find a suitable housing option for you.

It is very difficult to find a senior living community and move in one week. Do you really want to put your loved one through this?

Depending on your physical limitations, you may not qualify for independent living and may have to move into assisted living. You will find this out after a little research and visits to several communities.

Tip: The key is having good cognition as you age. Mentally sharp seniors can make their own decisions about future levels of care even when they are physically limited.

Choice 3: Move to a Continuing Care Retirement Community (CCRC)

If you have physical limitations, you may or may not qualify for a CCRC. Usually, seniors who move into independent living can manage entirely on their own. Many residents may use walkers on a temporary basis (as Dorothy did after her fall) or even on permanent basis but still be able to manage their daily routine on their own.

Because of Dorothy's mishap on the ice, Brian was forced to unexpectedly and quickly determine his mom's financial worth. Some parents are forthcoming with their financial situation and others are not. Often, adult children have to become sleuths to determine all the necessary factors to make a sound decision in the family's best interest. Brian is Dorothy's only child. If Brian had siblings, this situation might be even more complicated, since adult siblings rarely agree on elder care for their parents.

Do not delay for too long the decision to move into a CCRC as they require certain levels of assets and monthly income. You may exhaust your resources using home care before you know it. Brian is concerned about his mom's limited assets being eaten up by home care. Even though his mom owns her home, Dorothy's current assets barely qualify for a CCRC. Seniors are often shocked at how much and how quickly temporary care can deplete their savings. In the long run, moving into a CCRC is likely to be the last move you make as most CCRCs provide all the levels of care you will need as you age. Use my tips in earlier chapters to help you select a good community that will provide great care for you the rest of your life.

If Dorothy insists on long-term home care, what will Brian and Dorothy do when she runs out of money? If Dorothy uses up her financial resources on home care, she will be left only with the equity in her home. If she is forced to sell her home where will Dorothy live? She will not be able to move into a CCRC as the value of her home alone will not qualify her for a CCRC.

I am repeating an earlier tip again, because it is that important:

Tip: A CCRC typically has three or four levels of care on the same campus. They are designed to transition you to the next level of care. Staff is in place to make this happen. This is a part of their mission and what they do for residents on a daily basis.

Scenario C: for a couple, one cognitively competent and one with dementia or physical challenges

My in-laws, Amy and Bill, faced this situation just one year ago. Refer to the discussion in chapter 12, "In Denial and Waiting for a Crisis." Many couples find themselves suddenly in this predicament after their spouse has had a health crisis. The healthy spouse takes care of and compensates for the ill spouse.

Tip: Caring for a spouse with dementia or physical challenges can take a toll on the healthy spouse. In less than one year, my father-in-law's cognition greatly decreased because his social life ended when he became a full-time caregiver for his wife. He is physically worn out and mentally fatigued. Being a full-time caregiver is exhausting. A loving spouse has to become the chief cook, bottle washer, bather, driver, and medication administrator. And more!

Here are your choices:

Choice 1: Stay at home and bring in home care help

If you are not physically strong enough to help your spouse, home care can be a good short-term solution so you can continue to live in your home together. You may only need two shifts per week, which are usually four-hour minimum shifts each. Some spouses want to save the money and perform the care giving themselves.

My friend's Uncle Jack insisted he was strong enough to help his wife to the bathroom. A few weeks of this physical exertion took its toll on him and his back went out. Now he needs a caregiver too. He can't even walk the dog anymore.

If your spouse needs toileting or further assistance, then home care can become expensive. Around-the-clock care from a reputable company can run $18,000 a month or more.

Tip: Before you exhaust your resources, let's look at the other choices.

Choice 2: Move to a month-to-month rental facility

If one of you needs memory care for Alzheimer's or skilled nursing care because of a health crisis, such as a debilitating stroke, and the other spouse is well, you may not be able to stay together.

I am so sorry for the difficult situation you are in. I see this scenario daily. You may have taken a vow of "until death do you part," but in this case, you may still be married but physically apart. Unfortunately, spouses do not age at the same rate.

Tip: A healthy spouse may be able to move to an assisted living community with their spouse who needs assistance, so they can stay together. But a healthy spouse will not be able move to a skilled nursing community or secured memory care with their needy spouse.

What if you are the healthy spouse? Check out your options, based on your unwell spouse's needs. Use my tips from earlier chapters to find a good quality community that will provide for your spouse's needs. Hopefully, you will find a community that will help your spouse to thrive again or live the best possible quality of life given the situation.

Tip: If you are still maintaining your home, which has such expenses as upkeep and property taxes, the cost of a rental facility for your spouse on a monthly basis can deplete your assets quickly.

Double tip: A spouse can remain in a higher level of care for days, weeks, months, or years. My mom lived in assisted living for seven years, during which time she ran out of resources. You must be careful. Look at your situation now and determine what is best for your long-term finances. It may be best to split the assets with your spouse now. Check this with an attorney or financial advisor.

Choice 3: Move to a Continuing Care Retirement Community (CCRC)

If your spouse is in the early stages of dementia, Alzheimer's, or some type of physical challenge, you may or may not qualify for a CCRC.

If you don't meet the income requirements, a CCRC is not an option for you as a couple. Most couples sell their home in order to afford this choice.

Check out this option before you deplete your assets paying for home care or a rental facility. Some CCRCs may allow you to move into their community and permit care for your spouse in an independent apartment. Others may provide a discount for your spouse in a higher level of care.

Nine couples have recently shared with me why they were grateful for their decision to move into a CCRC. They all moved when they were healthy and fit. Living in a CCRC has ended up helping their families before, during, and after sudden healthcare crises. It is not that unusual in my world to have numerous family testimonials about how a CCRC supported these residents through ailments ranging from broken hips to knee replacements and the onset of dementia. The seniors and their families were grateful they made a decision to move before a crisis, even though all had been absolutely convinced they could live on their own before they moved.

Tip: A CCRC can help you navigate choppy waters as your spouse bounces back and forth to a hospital. They can provide all types of support from transportation for you to visit your spouse in the hospital to transitioning your spouse back to the CCRC after the medical crisis, including respite care in assisted living or their skilled nursing center. Many CCRCs have in-house care that can help you manage your ill spouse in your apartment on a temporary or even permanent basis. Ask a lot of questions when you are considering your move. Every CCRC is different and some do not provide skilled nursing care.

Double tip: Most seniors have a home to sell and use this to pay the one-time investment that CCRCs require. Ask if they offer a guarantee of care for you, and get that guarantee in writing. It puts a lot of risk on a CCRC to take on couples in this situation. So, if you have waited until this point in your life a CCRC may not even accept you and your unhealthy spouse, especially if you don't have a substantial monthly income.

Scenario D: for a couple when both have dementia (This section is also directed toward adult children who need to find an appropriate option for their parent(s) who have waited too long.)

Tips2Seniors.net

My in-laws, Bill and Amy, are in this situation now. Bill was fine until he deteriorated as a result of being a full-time caregiver for my mother-in-law. This effort accelerated his health decline. Unfortunately, despite my husband's and my advice, they have waited until they are out of options and the family is discussing what to do now. They have lost their ability to choose and now the family is forced to choose for them. Is this what you want for you and your family?

Even after family discussions with Bill and Amy, my father-in-law is convinced that he can continue providing the care for his wife. He has been her only caregiver for two years. Recently, he got lost driving home and had to ask for directions. Currently, he is confused about his bills. He believed that he was spending more money than he was bringing in, although he has had the same income stream for years. His macular degeneration and dementia are affecting his ability to reason and manage money and to drive.

My in-laws' adult children are in denial about their father's recent mental and physical decline. The children need to act quickly or both their mom and dad will be in jeopardy. If their father cannot remember his income, how can he remember to administer crucial medications and properly provide meals for them both?

Tip: Believe me, I know what you are going through. I have worked in senior housing for years and my own dear family struggles when reviewing long-term options for care. Children's arguments about care for their parents often cause dissention and stress in families. I am sure that you do not want to do this to your loved ones.

My own family is in this crisis and the children need to decide what to do. Here are the choices.

Choice 1: Stay at home and bring in home care help

When both people are cognitively challenged, they need someone else to manage their medications. Home care caregivers are not trained to provide this service. Therefore, home care is not a good option for a couple when both have dementia and need medication assistance.

Does your family situation resemble Bill and Amy's? If they insist on staying home, they will have to pay for a morning caregiver for four hours and an evening caregiver for four hours to do chores and make meals. Hiring caregivers for about eight hours a day costs around $6,000 a month. The cost would be $18,000 or more a month for around-the-clock care from a reputable agency. Ouch! This is a high price to pay for them to manage in their own home (still without any medication management.)

In their situation, who will manage the caregivers? Their oldest son, my husband, Chris, lives 1,000 miles away. Their only daughter lives about two hours away and has to take a ferry to get to them. Another son lives five hours away and doesn't drive. The third son does not have the personality to manage a caregiver.

 **Tip for adult children: Talk to your parents before they deplete their resources on short-term care options and try to get them to look at long-term solutions. Remember, you want to give your parents choices but their cognitive challenges may be preventing them from reasoning well.**

If you are a senior and still insisting that you are fine, keep reading.

Choice 2: Move to a month-to-month rental facility

- *Ten years ago*, my family discussed the *option* that both my in-laws could move to a retirement community. Amy said, "Yes" and Bill said, "No." Is this your situation too?
- *Two years ago*, we discussed the *possibility* that they could move to a community that offered independent living for him and assisted living for her. Amy said, "Yes" and Bill still said, "No."
- *One year ago*, we discussed the *need* for them to move to a community that offered independent living for him and assisted living for her. Amy said, "Yes" and Bill said, "I will wait until there is a crisis."

So here we are today and Bill refuses to move. What does he think a crisis is? Bill and Amy can't even remember that their long-distance son spent considerable time with them two weeks ago. Bill can no longer safely take care of his wife although he insists that he can. His own dementia and macular degeneration have limited his independence.

Ladies and gentlemen this is a crisis! Do you really want to wait for a crisis? If your answer is yes, then you have greatly limited your options.

My in-laws are no longer eligible for independent living. Both now need assisted living or assisted living with memory care. They no longer qualify for a CCRC.

Tip for adult children: Home care or an assisted living community can drain financial resources. Be smart and choose the best option for your parent, before their finances are depleted.

Double tip for adult children: You cannot force your parents to move. An assisted living community will not accept someone who is kicking and screaming, "No, no, no!"

This next section is for your adult loved ones to read.

What can you do when your parents refuse to move?

You have four choices, but they will depend on what your parental crisis entails. I hope you find some comfort in the fact that you are not alone. Remember that most of our parents, in-laws, or loved ones chose this crisis for themselves, because fear of change (leaving their home) right now is a greater fear than a health care crisis in the future. Here are your poor choices in crisis mode.

1. Let them live at risk in their homes, knowing you have done everything you can. This is a horrible solution, but you can't force a parent or loved one into a retirement community. Possibly, you or a home care worker can provide some support. Maybe it is the adult child who calls twice a day to see if the parents answer the phone. Pill dispensers for medications can help. Some loved ones call three times a day to remind parents to take their medications. Remember, your parents chose this. It is not your fault.

2. You bide your time and wait for a crisis. Then you put your parent some place under crisis conditions. You will have limited options. If your mom or dad ends up in skilled nursing care or a hospital, an assisted living can seem like a palace in comparison. A doctor can determine that they are not safe to live in their own home any longer and can dictate this choice, so you won't have to be the bad guy.

    Once their cognitive levels have deteriorated, it will be less expensive for your parents to live in a rental facility than it will be to bring in around the clock home care. It also takes the pressure off your managing their care. You will still need to go to the community where they live at least once a week (go on different days) to make sure all is well. Waiting for a crisis is a horrible solution. If you spoke with them and they understand they are waiting for a crisis, then they are responsible. Don't feel guilty.

3. Declare your parents incompetent and put them in a secured memory care or skilled nursing center (they need to have little cognitive ability in order to be eligible for this option). This is another horrible situation.

4. Move your mom or dad and tell them, "This is where you are living now." It is all prearranged between the family members and the community. This is typically only done for assisted living care or higher levels of care when the senior has severe dementia. This option can be very questionable, so go with your heart in your particular circumstance.
    After a fall my mom had become isololated from lack of mobility. This led to an increase in her dementia, erratic behavior, and she was taking her medications incorrectly. After

months of deliberation and family squabbles, my daughter took her grandma to lunch. My sister, husband, and I moved everything that was important to my mom into her new assisted living apartment. When my daughter brought my mom there after lunch, we told her that this was her new home. The staff gave my mom a lot of extra attention. We went through a very bumpy time, but within two weeks, she was thrilled with her new home. Sometimes seniors just can't face the details of moving, so doing it for them may be a good solution.

COMING SOON: *Senior Housing Options—for Your Parents* provides quick tips and support for baby boomer adult children whose parents are aging.

Conclusion

If a senior intentionally waits until a crisis, choices will be limited.

For seniors who can afford it, like my friend Alice, a widow with no children living nearby, a Continuing Care Retirement Community (CCRC) is the best option. It is also a great option for couples who can then stay together on the same campus. A CCRC will transition you to the next level of care when it is needed, taking that responsibility off your spouse or adult family member.

Alice chose home care. The caregiver was a friend of a friend. Alice fired her because their personalities did not mesh. Then a neighbor found a second caregiver who wanted to charge $20 an hour, "under the table." See chapter 3, "The Facts on Home Care." The neighbor said, "No way! Alice can only afford $15 an hour." The caregiver agreed, but Alice eventually fired that one too, because she thought she was stealing. Now, Alice's assets are depleted and she can't afford to live in her home any more. It is actually more economical for Alice to move. No more oil bill, no more lawn maintenance, no more housekeeper and caregiver bills. Because Alice did not plan ahead, her choices are now limited. Her only option is to move to a rental facility, because she was convinced that she could manage in her home and spent all her assets.

As dementia progresses, a rental facility can be a good option for seniors like my friend Alice or my in-laws with a good monthly income. But most rental facilities do not offer all levels of needed future care. Therefore, at some point you will need to move again. Who will help if your cognition is impaired? Just remember that rental facilities are under no obligation to help you find a good quality place where you will be happy and thrive. Their only obligation is to help you find a higher level of care, not necessarily the best place for you.

Home care is a Band-Aid fix that is best for short-term situations, such as recovering from a hospital stay. Long-term, around the clock home care requires an unlimited budget. You will also need loved ones or someone with power of attorney living nearby to manage your care on a daily basis when your cognition is impaired.

Please don't put your children in a situation where they are concerned for your well being. At some point your declining health, along with your inability to take your medications properly, can affect your capability of remaining independent. Your children then have no easy options and have to consider one of three choices, which entail "putting you some place."

Chapter 14
Conclusion From a Senior Living Expert and Loving Daughter

It has been heart wrenching for me to witness frail seniors, friends, and family struggling to remain in their home. Over my 16 year career in senior housing, thousands of seniors have said, "I want to stay in my home." At the same time I have seen and heard:

- Sons and daughters pleading with their parents to move to a safer and more supportive environment.
- Spouses who are completely worn-out caregivers.
- Lonely seniors who have lost their social connections because it is too much effort to leave their home or because they can no longer safely drive.
- Stubborn moms who call a loved one saying such things as, "I have no bread." "I am eating my last banana." "I took my last blood pressure pill yesterday." "Can you take me to the hairdresser." "Can you get me some groceries?"
- Seniors with dementia who understand they have memory loss.
- Seniors with dementia who are oblivious to their memory loss and how it affects those they love most.

- Paranoid seniors (one type of dementia) who feel their entire family is against them and have lost their grip on reality.
- Fearful seniors who recently got lost driving home.
- Adult children who have to call their parents twice a day to make sure they are okay.

Once a senior reaches their 70s or 80s, he or she is one fall away from a crisis. Some seniors can recover from a fall and others become permanently disabled. It's a roll of the dice and depends on your age, your health, and your bones.

By a senior's mid-80s, he or she has a 50 percent chance of developing dementia. It is an ugly disease, which has slowly eroded the minds of many whom I hold dear.

It is ultimately your choice to wait until a crisis and lose your ability to choose where you live *or* to plan ahead and choose how you will live in the future. You decide.

Do you want to just wait until they take you out feet first? Not very many seniors just die in their sleep. My own grandmother fell and was not found in her apartment for one week. This resulted in a hospital stay, followed by a permanent placement in a horrible skilled nursing home. Crises and emergencies are not fun, nor are they fair for you or your family.

Medication mismanagement can happen slowly. You are fine one day and then slowly over time your cognitive ability declines. It is like looking in the mirror everyday and not noticing you are aging.

Unfortunately, you may not realize that you missed a dose or that you overmedicated yourself until your health has deteriorated.

My mom was supposedly fully capable of dispensing her medications. Then her health declined rapidly over a six-month period. We did not discover until the day we moved her to assisted living that the majority of her pills were expired and she had not been taking the proper doses.

Boomer children have shared horror stories with me, relating how their parents have gone off the deep end from mismanaged medications. Some prescription medications can make you psychotic if you take too much. Nobody in his or her right mind ever wants to end up in a geriatric psychiatric ward. Please create a plan for your long-term care before you get to the point of wondering whether or not you have taken your medications for the day.

You need to determine whether or not you want to manage caregivers when you don't feel well. Isolation and memory loss both increase your vulnerability. Caregivers in your home can be great temporary companions, but let's face it, they are paid friends. Caregivers need to be managed and if they are not working out they need to be fired. This can be difficult for a single senior with dementia or a couple who both have dementia.

My friend Alice was recently diagnosed with dementia. Her neighbor has helped her to hire three caregivers because she was not eating regularly. In the last two months Alice has fired all of them. Now, her only choice is to move to a rental facility, because the upkeep of her home has become too costly. Alice has depleted her assets due to racking up credit card charges and overspending her income. Please make a decision before you become an Alice-like statistic.

My parents-in-law both have dementia and are currently in crisis. My father-in-law went from being a full-time caregiver for my mother-in-law to needing help himself. No one is managing their medications and both have dementia. They refuse to get help and they insist on staying in their home. They are not making good decisions because of their dementia. They can only live in the present moment and have lost the ability to plan ahead.

As my mother-in-law struggled with dementia, she would say, "Getting old is not for sissies!"

My mother planned ahead 16 years ago. She has had great social connectivity, excellent food, and a supportive environment for all these years. It was the smartest decision she made after my dad died and the best gift she could have given her children. She enjoyed the best eight years of her life in independent living. Then she had a fall and memory loss developed into dementia. Because she had planned ahead and researched her options, the next level of care was predetermined. My mom transitioned to assisted living, lived there for seven years and for the last 18 months has been in skilled nursing care. I am grateful for all the caregivers, nurses, and doctors who have supported her, so she can enjoy the best quality of life possible.

I wish you well and hope you make a decision to plan ahead. It is the best gift you can give to your children. If you don't have children, it is even more important to plan ahead.

Here's to finding the perfect solution for your next chapter of life.

Diane Twohy Masson

P.S. Do you want to learn what it's like for a spouse or your adult children trying to help you as you age?

COMING SOON: *Senior Housing Options—for Your Parents* provides quick tips and support for baby boomer adult children whose parents are aging.

Your Senior Housing Options

About the Author

The author spent two years exploring senior housing options with her mom before finding the ideal Continuing Care Retirement Community for her mom. After enjoying eight successful years in an independent living setting, her mom suffered a fall and the onset of dementia. This daughter helped transition her to assisted living—in the nick of time. Seven years later, even this expert struggled making the dramatic decision to move her mom long distance into a skilled nursing community.

Diane Twohy Masson has worked in Senior Housing since 1999 and is an award-winning certified aging services professional (CASP) with a BS in business management and a minor in marketing from Central Washington University. She can share behind the scenes insider tips and advice after mystery shopping 300 senior living communities. Diane and her teams have helped thousands of seniors move into various styles of senior living, but she learned that the hardest move is helping your own parent.

Diane Twohy Masson is the best-selling author of *Senior Housing Marketing—How to Increase Your Occupancy and Stay Full*, available at Amazon.com with a five-star rating. The book is required reading at George Mason University as part of its marketing curriculum. In this book, the author developed a sales method with 12 keys to helping senior living providers increase their occupancy.

She enjoys public speaking, golfing, traveling, Disneyland, bird watching, writing, hiking, camping, reading, scripture study, and spending time with her family.

For more information:

Website: www.Tips2Seniors.com
Blog: www.marketing2seniors.net/the-blog-for-seniors/
Twitter: @tips2seniors
E-mail: diane@Tips2Seniors.com
Linked In: www.linkedin.com/pub/diane-masson/21/580/57

11845713R00126